ESCAPE FROM KABUL

ALSO BY ENAKSHI SENGUPTA

The Silk Route Spy

ESCAPE FROM KABUL

A True Story of Escape and Survival

ENAKSHI SENGUPTA

HARPER
NON-FICTION
An Imprint of HarperCollins *Publishers*

First published in India by Harper Non-Fiction 2025
An imprint of HarperCollins *Publishers*
HarperCollins *Publishers* India, Cyber City,
Building 10-A, Gurugram, Haryana – 122002, India
www.harpercollins.co.in

2 4 6 8 10 9 7 5 3 1

P-ISBN: 978-93-6989-128-3
E-ISBN: 978-93-6989-601-1

Typeset in 11 pt/15 Adobe Garamond Pro
by HarperCollins *Publishers* India Pvt. Ltd

Printed and bound at
Thomson Press (India) Ltd

FSC
www.fsc.org
MIX
Paper | Supporting responsible forestry
FSC® C010615

This book is produced from independently certified FSC® paper
to ensure responsible forest management.

HarperCollins *Publishers*, Macken House, 39/40 Mayor Street Upper, Dublin 1, D01 C9W8, Ireland

To my late husband, Vijay Kapur,
and my parents, Mira and Naresh Ranjan Sengupta:
I am because you are

Prologue

Escape is a small six-letter word but it holds immense potential as it contains the meaning of emancipation, the possibilities of new horizons, and freedom from painful shackles, both physical and mental.

When I lost a loved one, I wanted to escape, to find an easy way to run away from all that was familiar. An opportunity came in the form of a job that entailed teaching students in Kabul. It would require me to help young men and women realize their dreams by imparting knowledge on starting a new business. However, soon, the excitement of travel subsided and it was replaced by the apprehension of *What if I don't come back? What if I am abducted or killed, or an even worse predicament awaits me?* I tried to discuss this with people to gather their opinion and heard strong reactions like, *Are you suicidal? Are you in your senses? Who goes there? Let this be our last supper then. I hope you have a nominee mentioned in your bank account* … etc.

I left for Kabul with these not-so-encouraging words ringing in my ears. The airport was formidable, with towering men (literally) looking down on me. Then I heard kind voices and kind hands reaching out to help. 'Ma'am, please allow us to help you with your luggage.' 'Ma'am, may I help you with pushing your trolley?' 'Do you have a car, or should we drop you at your destination?' Kindness was pouring out from strangers. Awkward in my thick jacket, trying to hold on to my files and laptop, and managing a head scarf for the first time, I mustered up some courage and smiled and nodded at the kind and helpful souls.

As the vehicle meandered through the roads and bylanes, I completely fell in love with the white flowing beard of the grandfather standing at the bus stop with his grandson, the beautiful couple who were matching their pace and walking down the road, the pretty young girl adjusting her backpack, the boy with his long thick hair who arched his eyebrows to look at my car, those green and blue eyes staring at me—all so beautiful. The cart full of red apples or pomegranates and colourful sweets made me feel as if I were driving through a garden. This city has so much to offer—and all of it is so little known to the outside world.

A year passed and then those sentences started doing the rounds, 'US forces have withdrawn' and 'NATO forces are not going to support …' The word 'escape' had now become ever so meaningful. It was the only thing that people in Afghanistan could now think of. I spent sleepless nights, staying awake till 3 a.m., feeling sick to the core when my colleague expressed his fear of being beheaded, or when my student hid in the toilet to attend his online classes. I was frantically searching for a way to take my students to my country or to someplace safe. I cried with my female students when they expressed their anguish about being caught studying and then punished. Their anguish, fear and palpitations were mine. I wanted nothing but a way to escape for all.

After it all came to an end, even now I can't forget what those lovely people of Afghanistan had gone through and are still going through. I do hope that this wonderful country becomes a symbol of peace and prosperity someday. As you begin reading this book, do send a small prayer for these beautiful people of Afghanistan.

Introduction

The August sun in Kabul was overbearing. Winter was lurking around the corner, but the sun had decided to come down with its full force. Perhaps it was cognizant of the fact that in a couple of months, it would be far from its usual self, dying a slow death, giving way to months of bleak snowfall.

The few green grass blades in the adjacent field were putting up a tough fight against those already yellowed; it was their last attempt to remain alive. The air was thick with a putrid, smoky smell. The routine doesn't break, the routine doesn't know where to end, and hence classes were taking place as usual in hot and humid classrooms where the whizzing fan was making the summer more tedious to bear, circulating the stale air mixed with the smell of sweat and languor. The faces of the students were red and marked with rashes as they were incessantly wiping their faces to combat the heat, making it worse. Everything and everyone looked sleepy and steeped in the lazy ambiance, which seemed to be dragging itself into a stupor.

Dr Catherine or Cathy, a frail-looking, petite lecturer in her mid-forties, with a tight bun on her head and a pair of spectacles on the bridge of her nose, was trying hard to explain the Geneva Convention to a bunch of sleepy students. They looked tired; the heat, coupled with the night-long power cuts, was not allowing them to rest at night. Dr Cathy was also feeling drained due to the heat and lethargy in the air. However, she was trying her best to make the topic interesting. She wanted her students to participate in the upcoming inter-departmental debate. Her students had always lost out to those from law or management.

Suddenly, Ahmad Qadri's large frame blocked the light coming from the ajar classroom door. Dr Catherine found it strange that the security guard, who never stepped inside the classroom, especially when class was in progress, was standing right there.

'Yes, Qadri, do you need something? Tell me?'

'Madam, you finish class, Watson Sahib calls you, you come now?'

'Now? I am in the class; we still have around forty minutes to go.'

'But Sahib calls you, everyone go, everyone five or ten minutes, Sahib speaks.'

'Okay, okay, I am coming with you. Students, I guess we need to end today's lesson. Let me know if you're facing any issues. You know how to reach me: drop me an email. See you all in the next class. See you the day after.'

Then, turning to the security guard, she said, 'Okay, Qadri, let's go, let's see why your Sahib is calling all of us today. Maybe he will give us a promotion or extra money, what do you think?'

Dr Catherine joked as she picked up her bag and stepped outside the classroom. Panting heavily, she strode on, matching her step with this giant of a security guard.

Qadri was a serious man, and his post as a security supervisor strictly prohibited him from talking to the faculty members or the staff; hence, he just managed to muster up a smile of politeness and in the next instant drew a deadpan face as they both headed to the university president's room.

Dr Watson, an elderly man in his early seventies, was lost in paperwork when Dr Catherine noisily pulled the chair in front of him and waited for his instruction to sit down. Dr Watson looked up, adjusting his glasses, and said, 'Good, good, that you are here, Cathy. I needed to speak to all of you individually. Do you want a cup of tea?'

Dr Cathy shook her head, indicating a no; she didn't want to drink a cup of tea just before the lunch break. She had been having a bout of acidity since last week—possibly because of the oily food at the canteen—so she would avoid drinking tea in the afternoon.

Dr Watson was a kind-looking man. He was balding from the front and was bespectacled, which gave him a fatherly look. Besides, he was paternalistic in his way of handling the Anglo-American University of Kabul. He had worked as a political attaché for the US government and had been stationed in Kazakhstan, Armenia and Uzbekistan for almost three decades. With a master's in political science and anthropology, he had a fair understanding of the geopolitical scenario of Central Asia and was aware of the religious and political sensitivities of this region. His wife, who had worked as a psychologist and counsellor, worked with him on campus. Both of them taught a course or two. On his retirement from government service, he wanted to spend time with his daughter in Hawaii, but one of his close aides offered him the job as the president of the university. The offer was lucrative, and he took it up without much hesitation. He enjoyed what he was doing as much as he enjoyed playing with his dog and baking a cake in his spare time. There was a rumour that he might retire next year, although it was not confirmed.

Dr Watson pushed the paperwork aside, took his glasses off and kept them on the table before he reclined on his chair and sighed.

'Cathy, I am telling you the same thing that I have told Dr Sharma, Dr Cullins and the rest of us who are stationed here in Kabul. Things do not look good. The situation here, in Afghanistan, is worsening even as we speak.

'I was apprehensive of this as the US forces withdrew. I knew it would be a matter of time before I needed to call all of you, one by one, and talk about this. I am being told that the Taliban forces are advancing rapidly, and every day, a new province is falling into their hand. It is just going to be a couple of days before they capture Kabul. I mean, the power most likely will be handed over to them; they don't even need to capture anything by force. I don't know the exact repercussions of all this. I am relying on sources that can update me accordingly and tell me what is to be done next. The Taliban have not been favourable towards us in the past, and I don't expect them to be. You must have read about the attack on the campus and the abductions of our faculty members in 2010 and 2012. I don't want all that to be repeated. We should plan towards evacuating the campus and reconvening at a later date when things become normal, and I hope they do.'

Catherine sat listening to Dr Watson. She nervously fidgeted with her scarf under the table, determined not to display her nervousness to anyone. 'So, what do you advise us to do now? To flee, just escape, leaving the students, semester, everything behind?' gulped Catherine, her voice quivering as she spoke, with a tinge of irritation and impatience.

'No, Cathy, I am not asking anyone to flee. But plan your moves, we still have some time in hand. Get your tickets, pack your bags and be on the next flight out.'

Cathy looked worried. She kept quiet for a few seconds, lowering her eyes and picking at the hem of her scarf again.

Dr Watson cleared his throat and added, 'I know you don't have a place of your own, and you don't want to go and stay with your mother. I completely understand that. But this is a temporary arrangement; we will regroup somewhere again soon. The university is going to carry on. I will not allow it to succumb to such forces.' Dr Watson did sound very emotional.

Dr Cathy got up. As she was about to leave the room, she turned around to thank him, 'One last question, will we continue to get our salary? You know I hardly have any savings, or should I look for a job elsewhere? I cannot afford to sit at home; I have drained all my savings trying to save both my marriages. You know that.'

'Salaries will be paid; we have some reserves. Don't worry about it at this point. I will look into it,' Dr Watson assured her.

Dr Watson's assurance did very little to assuage her troubled mind. Cathy walked slowly towards the university canteen, her head down, adjusting her glasses on the bridge of her nose. There were lots of things that were weighing on her mind at that moment, the foremost being: she could get her flight tickets as instructed, but go where? She was exhausted. It was visible in the way she dragged her feet to the canteen. Questions and troublesome thoughts kept lingering in her mind. Who would be willing to welcome her into their houses?

She had been divorced twice. The first was one initiated by her as she could no longer endure the mental and physical torture by her husband, and the second one was a bigger disaster. The man whom she married out of love had drained her of her savings and thrown her out of the house. The trauma had left her broken and tired. She needed time to heal. She thought that teaching in Afghanistan, away from all that was once familiar, would help her to heal.

Now that she had been asked to leave the campus, she kept thinking about where to go. One possible option was to stay with her mother or her sister for the time being. But she realized that it was an illusion of an option. Her mother and sister were judgemental and blamed her for her two failed marriages. She felt claustrophobic around them as they cornered her with their never-ending advice as to how best she should handle her life, and requesting them to stop had little effect on them. She could barely be around them, and that usually happened within a day or two after her arrival.

She started thinking about going away. She just had her blue suitcase and a backpack that would not take her long to pack.

She wondered if she would get a chance to say goodbye to her students ... probably not, as there was hardly much time, as she had heard.

Reaching the canteen, she served herself some pasta, but suddenly she was not hungry anymore. The pasta looked insipid and stale, or was she imagining it?

As she turned around, she saw Dr Anjali Sharma sitting at one of the tables. Dr Sharma had joined the university a couple of months ago. She was usually a very quiet person with a forlorn look; she didn't speak or mix with the others. She was rarely seen at social gatherings or evening bonfires. Cathy had heard that she had lost her husband last year; perhaps she was still struggling with her grief.

But today, Cathy needed someone to talk to. She took her plate over to where Dr Sharma was sitting and asked politely, 'May I?' She had never noticed earlier that Dr Sharma had a very sweet and charming smile; she smiled and moved aside, making space for Dr Cathy to sit down.

'Did Dr Watson talk to you? He spoke to me.'

'Yes,' said Dr Sharma, almost in a whisper.

'Are you going back to India? Which city?'

'There is only one flight to Delhi. I will get the ticket and then go and stay with my mother. Since he left, I don't feel like going back to our apartment. All his belongings are still lying around. I didn't have the heart to donate them.'

'I can understand,' mumbled Cathy.

'Oh! I didn't know you lost your husband, too. I am so sorry!'

'Well, they are lost for sure. I had two bad marriages. They are living, but sometimes I wish those monsters were dead. Maybe memories would have been better; it would have been only grief and not grief mixed with hatred. It is different, you know.'

'Yes … I want to hate him. I try to remember our fights, our disagreements. I feel grief with hatred would be easier to digest. But all his memories are painfully loving and full of care and happiness. That is not helping me; it doesn't allow me to live,' Dr Sharma's voice choked, tears welling up in her large eyes as she spoke to Dr Cathy.

Cathy tried to divert her attention from her grief and changed the conversation, 'Did your embassy contact you? Are you in touch with them? What are they saying?'

'Yes, I did. As soon as I came to Kabul, I contacted them. We needed to register our details, and I did that. Then a squadron leader got in touch with me. A Captain Varma asked about my well-being, whether I was comfortable here, etc. We do have a WhatsApp group, you know. They keep sending updates there. So far, I have not received anything significant. I will inform you if they do.'

'Ah! Your embassy seems to be very organized. The WhatsApp group is a good idea; I wish mine had one too,' remarked Dr Cathy.

They both kept quiet for the rest of the meal, occasionally looking up and smiling weakly. Heaviness was weighing on them and all around them. Both finished their lunch and moved toward their office building. For the first time, it seemed they were bonding, or perhaps it was that earlier, no one had made any attempt to befriend the other.

As they were about to enter their respective offices, Cathy turned around and said, 'Dr Anjali, have you seen Kabul city?

Today is Thursday; tomorrow is Friday, which is a day off for us. Do you want to go to the only 5-star hotel here, Hotel Arina? They have a good beauty parlour. Maybe we could both get a touch-up and a haircut? Then we can go for some food and shopping. What do you think?'

'That sounds lovely. I have barely gone out since I came here. Do you think the security director will give us permission and a vehicle to go out of campus, now that things are not looking very good?'

'Leave that to me. Braddy is a good friend; he might even join us at the restaurant. I will let you know. We will go around midday. It will be easier then as the streets are less crowded.'

◈

As both women, who were very different and yet similar in a way, reached their respective offices, they had the same thought—the impending certainty of losing their jobs and going back to a home they had escaped from. Their refuge was going to be taken away. Cathy didn't want the thought to linger and ruin her day, and she was already looking forward to an outing with Dr Anjali. Anjali was also happy; maybe she could find a friend in Cathy, and she would also get to see the city.

As soon as Cathy settled down in her office, the door opened and was closed with a loud bang. Nadia, who was in the final year of her BBA programme, walked in in an agitated state. Cathy had been apprehensive for quite some time that something was not right with this star student at the university, mainly after her marriage. However, Cathy didn't want to broach the subject unless the student herself brought it up.

'Doctor! You need to take me with you; I heard that the Taliban are coming. This is going to be a living hell. I am presently staying in one. I still have the respite of coming out every day as I am earning some money. You know that after my classes, I work with Dr Nancy as a part of the work-study programme. We are setting up the entrepreneurship club. This is helping me to earn money, and I am spared from staying with that brute for the entire day and night. But after this, I will be confined to the room. I will die if that happens. He will kill me. I can't endure it anymore. Please, Madam, take me with you. I will do anything for you. You do need house help, don't you?'

Cathy got up and hugged her tightly, 'Hush, hush, don't talk of dying. Life is still beautiful. Go back to your class, and we will talk about this later. Go now, wash your face and run back.'

Nadia went back to her classroom very quietly with her head down, adjusting her scarf and her backpack as she walked down the corridor. She was in a contemplative mood.

Everyone knew about Nadia's life at home. No matter how much concealer and foundation she put on her face, like many, Cathy could see the tell-tale signs of domestic violence. She had been through them, too, and those black and blue marks didn't go unnoticed by her.

Cathy sat down once again with a thud. The world is becoming unbearable, with so much cruelty and misery all around.

She didn't feel like correcting the pile of exam papers in front of her. Everything felt so fragile and meaningless, she decided to call it a day. She took her bag and slowly started walking towards her container, numbered 301, her designated room since last year. The shipping containers were kept in rows and had been made into a single-storeyed apartment, and the university tried to make it as comfortable as possible with modern equipment and appliances. Today, they appeared bleak and lifeless in Cathy's eyes.

The sun was setting, and it cast a shadow of gloom. It had painted everything a shade of pale gold and yellow as it decided to go to the other side of the world for the time being.

Zohra, who had recently joined the registrar's department, met Dr Catherine just when she was about to push the heavy iron gate that segregated the faculty quarters from the rest of the university. Zohra was from Toronto and, in her Canadian drawl, wanted to know whether the buzz of emptying the campus was true. 'Do you have a minute to spare? I just heard from someone that we are evacuating the campus. Is that true? When are we supposed to leave?'

Cathy assumed that the same thought of losing her job weighed heavily on the mind of this young girl. She turned around and placed her hand on Zohra's hand and gave her an assuring pat, 'Don't worry, my dear, the president said that it will be business as usual; nothing is going to change—apart from the location, maybe.'

Zohra opened her mouth to say something but then stopped abruptly. She decided not to go ahead and smiled in return and said, 'Thank you for letting me know, and I wish you a restful evening.' Saying this, she quickly disappeared amidst the trees.

As Cathy was entering the enclosed area for the expat housing, she spotted Fawzia from the canteen. Fawzia was hobbling back home; after a while, she rested on her crutches to wipe her face with her head scarf. Her job in the canteen was backbreaking, and with one leg and a crutch, it was rather difficult to stand and stir the broth or cut vegetables. But Alhamdulillah, she could only be grateful to God for being her provider and giving her a job at the university canteen. She could earn a living and feed herself and her son.

Without the job, she would be sitting at a busy road crossing and begging. She was too proud to do that, although a handicapped divorcee in Kabul could not think of an alternate arrangement for earning her livelihood. Her family failed to support her. She saw Dr Catherine going back to her quarters. She stopped to tell her, 'Salam, Dr Sahiba, food good? You like?'

Cathy smiled, raised her thumb and said, 'Very good, *tashakkur.*'

Both of them were struggling to survive and shared a special bond, although they were far from being similar. Their eyes met; they smiled at each other and decided to go on their designated paths, both returning home after a day's work.

The evening chugged towards nightfall; an eerie silence engulfed the campus that seemed to sweep at the door of every container where people were busy poring over their computers looking for a cheap flight back home.

A question mark was silently moving in front of every door, stealthily, trying to find the answer for tomorrow. Would the city fall? Would they create mayhem and chaos, killing everyone who looked different from them or opposed them?

No one knew what tomorrow or the day after held. When they went to bed, everyone murmured a prayer, hoping that they might live to see their loved ones.

Even Cathy wished that she could meet her mother and her sisters once more. Apprehensions and trepidations hung from the streetlights, dancing in their glory, as they had the answer that no one had—the vision of an unpleasant time ahead.

Part I

KHANOUMA: THE WOMEN

Cathy

Cathy drew her dry and flaky knees close to her chest and hugged them tightly in an attempt to gather all the warmth she could find. She needed a tight hug; someone who could take all her sorrow away and assure her that everything was going to be alright, but there was no one in this desolate apartment besides her. There was a thick mist of emptiness that engulfed her.

She was in a lot of pain and was scared. She felt as if a boulder had knocked her over and she had been ripped and bloodied from inside. A gnawing hole seemed to have formed where her heart used to be. The heart of a little girl, the heart of a lover, the heart that was pink and throbbing; nothing remained now, just a black gaping hole.

She spotted an old injury on her knee and tried hard to dig at it and peel the scab. When did she hurt her knee? She had no clue. She continued picking at it till the scab came out. She tossed the dry purple skin on the floor. A drop of fresh blood oozed out, which she rubbed with her sleeves. The burning sensation did nothing to soothe her.

The stream of tears streaking down her cheeks didn't seem to stop. Sometimes it flowed, sometimes in drops, waiting for a while on her high cheekbones, and sometimes it settled as a shimmering drop just above her parched and cracked lips. It kept coming, and no matter how many attempts were made to wipe it away, it just wouldn't stop.

She looked awful—dirty and unkempt, which was so unbecoming for her. Her hair was dry and matted and tied in a messy bun. Her blouse slid down from her shoulder, faltering at her raised shoulder bone. She must have lost a lot of weight in these two months, after having suffered from the COVID infection, being thrown out of her house with no proper job or livelihood to support herself.

She didn't care anymore; she was not bothered about her weight or her well-being. She secretly wished that she was dead and gone. She hadn't had a proper meal in a while now, no bath, maybe she hadn't even brushed her teeth and combed her hair, she did not know anymore. She retrieved one of her wine bottles from under the bed, which was empty.

She looked at it with a bemused smile and then, laughing loudly, she cried out, 'Oh, my dear bottle, you, too, are empty like me, we are like each other!' She kissed the bottle lightly and allowed it to roll on the floor once again.

She picked up her phone and stared at it with blurry eyes, blinking to adjust her foggy vision. She frantically searched for a missed call or a message from Ian, but there was none, nothing at all. Her nineteen missed calls had gone unanswered. Her threatening messages to commit suicide were unheeded, and her plea for him to come back had not even been read. She looked at the mess that was around her; all her belongings were strewn on the bed.

She had lost everything except for some dresses, a picture or two and a few useless trinkets of shells and beads in a tiny box. This was all she had now. Here she was: the much-respected Dr Murray, a member of the leadership team of a large university, sitting on a bed, unfed, unkempt, abandoned, howling like a teenager over her lost lover, her second husband.

Peeping out of the debris and relics of her past, which lay piled up in a heap on her bed, was the photograph she and Walter had clicked decades ago when they were high school buddies.

She had destroyed all his photographs after their bitter divorce, but somehow, she couldn't throw this one away; perhaps this was the first photograph of them together. How happy they looked; Walter was holding her hand tightly, and she was almost blushing.

Childhood romance had blossomed into real love. As the years progressed, two youngsters who had grown up loving each other spun their fairy tale and got married. They were a young couple in love, and they had dreamt of a nice house, holidays in a beach resort, a couple of children and a perfect English family complete with a dog.

However, cracks started appearing in this fairy tale when Walter returned from Iraq as a mental wreck, a shadowy ghost of his former self, after serving in the Staffordshire Regiment. The bright young man was replaced by a lost man with a forlorn look and pain in his eyes.

He was suffering from post-traumatic stress disorder, which he was reluctant to admit or seek medical help for, and he was often prone to violence and rage because of that. She was reminded of the fact that he never took up a job after that. He just sat on the sofa and kept drinking all day; he refused to even open the curtains or let sunlight enter their clammy and musty room.

He seemed to be an empty shell, and she was left all alone in the marriage, managing her job as a teaching assistant and doing her PhD at the same time. He was there physically, but his soul and mind seemed to be wandering in some lanes of Baghdad, searching for his friends in a ditch or running to seek cover.

He would wake up in the middle of the night screaming violently and sweating profusely. He would wake up flailing his arms and gasping for air, and he would keep shaking his head and murmuring to himself. He would avoid company and make excuses not to attend parties or social gatherings. Any successful attempt at securing a job for him would fail in one or two days when he usually picked up a fight, abused people and was thrown out.

She broke into uncontrollable sobs once again as she remembered how he had kicked her violently when she was in the advanced stages of her pregnancy and they had lost their child. It was raining heavily that night. Her tears stopped at the corners of her eyes. She was blank and numb with pain in her body and her soul.

Nothing ever healed the pain of her child dying in her womb, her womb shattered by the kick of the father of her child. Doctors told her she could never become a mother again; she was impaired for life by the only love of her life, her own Walter.

Her thin, bony frame shook as she tried not to remember that dreadful night. That was the last thread, and it snapped with her child dying inside her because of the violent kicks of the father. They showed her the bloody mass, which could have blossomed into a beautiful child, in a kidney tray.

Walter had become a monster, and his pledges to change himself and his crying did not affect Cathy. She had turned cold and her heart had transformed into stone. She didn't care for him or anyone else. The divorce was bitter and drained her of all her savings and exhausted her mentally.

Walter tried to accuse her of cheating on him, denying the fatherhood of the child. However, all came to rest after eight months of incessant struggle. Both outside and in the courtroom. She lost her job, took a leave of absence from pursuing her doctorate and was financially broke.

Chris, a friend of Walter and Cathy, was still serving in Iraq as a mercenary soldier. He had contacts with the political leaders and the who's who of the newly rebuilt society in Iraq. He managed to get her a job at an international university, which had just started its operation in a bright and beautiful campus in the broken city of Baghdad.

The pay was good as it factored in hardship costs and perks to suit someone working in a so-called dangerous country. Besides, she had something to look forward to: she needed to run away from her familiar surroundings, gather her courage, feel confident once again and rebuild her career and her savings.

Her mother and her sisters opposed this move, but she knew that her struggles were her own, and no one was really beside her. Their advice, warnings and newspaper clippings depicting violence in Iraq remained unheeded.

The campus was remote, away from the main city, and the journey to the airport took more than two hours due to the hilly terrain and checkpoints after every fifteen minutes. She didn't mind; she was looking forward to this part of her life with enthusiasm.

The barrenness of the place reflected her soul; she found some kind of kinship with the land as she looked at the dirty, dusty tracks on the hills. The place had no hope, no flowers blossoming, no green grass to cover the dust. It was like her; she was just surviving as she had to. A forlorn look crossed her face whenever she put her hand on her belly, the warmth that no child will ever seek.

The place where she was hosted by the university in the initial days had only one decent hotel belonging to a leading chain. She started frequenting the coffee shop for a sandwich, a steak or a hot croissant, as food in the university canteen was not to her taste.

One day, while she was complaining about her eggs Benedict, which was too runny, the chef was called, and that is when she met Ian Dubois. There was an instant chemistry between them; at least that was what she felt when their eyes met for the first time.

She was immediately drawn to his boyish charm, his blue eyes and even his rough, ginger-coloured curly hair tied in a small ponytail. His smile seemed to light up the whole place. She saw a tiny glimmer of hope that penetrated her heart; perhaps this smile would again reignite lost love.

A faint smile broke on her tear-soaked face as she remembered the day she had seen him. She picked up the blue-shelled pendant from her trinket box. This was the very first gift that Ian had given her. She still remembered that he insisted on putting it on her while she was holding her hair up with her left hand. He traced his finger all around her neck and kissed the nape, saying, 'Allow me, mademoiselle.'

She was charmed, she swooned. Love was coming back into her life, or was she dreaming? She kept twirling the pendant in her hand, her eyes still blurry with tears. Those days would never come back; she was now left alone, cold and without love.

Mindlessly, she touched her wedding gown that was lying crumpled on the bed beside her suitcase. The sequins and stones sewn on it pricked her finger, and she recoiled immediately. Her mind was playing tricks with her as she compared the dress to her rough, painful marriage.

This was the only dress she had liked in Iraq; she didn't want the Cinderella kind of gown she had worn for her first wedding. This wedding was meant to be simple, without much paraphernalia, just the two of them with some caring friends.

She picked up the phone again and dialled his number, and this time it rang. 'Please, please, Ian, pick up the phone, for heaven's sake, pick it up at least once, talk to me … please, I beg of you,' she kept mumbling to herself.

He did pick it up, but his voice was heavy and groggy, 'Didn't I tell you not to disturb me? Can't your dull brain understand simple English? Some doctorate you are! Wondered who gave you that degree, you are one dumb b***h, aren't you?'

'But … Ian, hear me out … I have nowhere to go, no money. Have mercy on me; think of all the lovely times we spent together. I am your wife. I love you and always will, please, Ian.'

'Go to hell for all I care. Soon you will not be my wife, you are a bl****y pain. Wonder what I was thinking when I married your ugly self. Hated you then and hate you now. Go back to your old lovers, that pretty boy from South America who taught English in that useless university and shared your apartment. Did he dump you, too? Good, you deserve it.'

He disconnected the line. She sat staring at nothing, the phone was still in her hand.

It had been a whirlwind romance for a year, and she had moved into his hotel room within a couple of months. He was the sweetest man she had ever encountered. What more would a woman want than breakfast in bed, wine in the evening, kisses and caresses throughout the day? Whenever they were together, it was passionate lovemaking at night after his dinner duty was over.

She was in seventh heaven; she had to pinch herself to believe that she could be so lucky. Then, one Friday, when they both had their day off and were still entwined in bed, Ian looked at her lovingly and said, 'Are you ready for a surprise?'

'What's more, you have been surprising me throughout the night, my lovely.'

Ian propped up his pillow, took out a small box and opened it. It had a small pearl ring in it. 'Will you marry me, my fair lady? Your poor chef could only afford a pearl and not a diamond, but someday he will.'

Cathy gasped; she was not expecting this at all. She sat up on the bed, not bothering to cover her modesty. She was too emotional to speak; she choked.

'Are you sure, Ian? I have told you everything. I cannot become a mother.'

'Ah! Who wants those pests running around and messing up my kitchen? Will you marry me, Dr Catherine?'

'Yes, yes, I will,' and they were once again lost in their world of kissing and making love to each other.

Ian was half English and half French. They decided to have their marriage in England, where Cathy's family and friends could join them. They both had to apply for leave and plan everything, and this was when they both decided to buy this silver dress with sequins and a plunging neckline.

The dress fitted her perfectly, enhancing her curvaceous figure. Ian joked that he couldn't wait to see her in that dress, and then out of that dress. Both wanted to host a simple wedding in Cornwall, inviting a few friends and family members.

A villa was booked. Cathy looked ravishing, shining like a star against the blue sea. Ian displayed his creativity, hanging lanterns from the tree and placing lavender flowers on every table. The menu was whipped up with foie gras, fresh salmon, lobster and calamari, accompanied by fresh lavender pudding. They had a generous supply of red and white wine to go with the seafood menu.

The couple decided to stay back in Cornwall to enjoy their honeymoon. For Cathy, the honeymoon had started a year back in Iraq, and it seemed endless. She secretly wished that it would continue for a very long time.

Soon, it was time to go back to Iraq and resume their jobs, and that is when Ian came up with his plan, which he had been working on for a long time, but Cathy had no inkling about it. Before he shifted to Baghdad, Ian was in India and had fallen in love with Goa. He wanted to start a bed-and-breakfast there and had been in discussion with some people he had met on his last visit to India. He had seen a very pretty villa near Anjuna beach. Since the owners stayed in Australia and were not really interested in maintaining it, the price was low.

Ian, lying on a couch with his head on Cathy's lap, said, 'Let's not go back to Iraq anymore and risk our lives. Let's pool our money, buy this villa and turn it into a little guest house for select customers. You can help me with the design and even work on promoting it with me. We will have a very peaceful life, and the beaches will give you the right kind of tan and enhance your beauty.'

Cathy was living her fairy tale in a perfect marriage with a loving husband and lots of romance; she was willing to go to Mars or the moon with him, and she yielded very fast. She pulled out all her savings and gave them to Ian, and they resigned from their jobs and headed to Goa. She was no longer the professor or administrator that she used to be and gave up her academic career just to be with him, helping him run the establishment.

The paperwork was endless, the house was dilapidated and the labourers were very difficult to manage. But they sailed through everything, and in six months, they had a beautiful little bungalow with twenty rooms. Friends started spreading the word around, Cathy's social media skills helped, and they were running at full capacity when the COVID pandemic hit.

Within a month, the guests disappeared, barring three or four of them who were long-staying guests and had nowhere to go. Money was dwindling fast, and soon, the once-beautiful romance turned sour in the mire of counting bills, payouts and maintenance.

Ian wanted to withdraw the last penny out of Cathy's bank as he felt that an outdoor wedding venue could be a way to salvage the situation. He wanted the garden to be appropriately decorated with a shed and seating arrangements. Cathy's protests soon disappeared in her attempt to make the marriage work.

Things were again looking up till she caught Ian in a compromising position with their long-staying Spanish guest, Veronica, one night.

Fights turned ugly, and once again, her days of horror with physical and mental abuse came back.

Cathy had fresh tears in her eyes as she recollected the way he had shouted at her.

'I should never have married you. You are a discarded piece of s**t. Men come into your life, and they get fed up with you. Look at your first husband and that Latino kid in Iraq. Don't tell me I don't know why he was sharing the apartment with you. You are nothing but a speck of dirt. You deserve to be on the roadside, kicked out of the house ...'

Cathy couldn't take it anymore. That very night, she threw some clothes in a suitcase and stormed out of the house.

She checked into a cheap hotel for the night and then rented a small apartment. And here she was, sitting on her bed, pleading with Ian to take her back into his life and trying to make her marriage work.

She wiped her tears away and went to the washroom to wash her face; her reflection in the mirror scared her. Dark circles, pale, blotchy skin, unwashed hair and reeking, ill-fitting clothes. As she looked into the mirror, she remembered—she was a fighter.

Her stomach growled; she needed to eat something and think with a calmer mind. She fixed herself a sandwich and a cup of tea.

She weighed her options: to go back to her mother—which was not the most pleasant thing to do—or to find a job. She dialled Chris's number; he would always show up as her saviour in times like these. He was the one who had arranged a job for her in Iraq after her bitter divorce from her first husband. Chris started the conversation with light-hearted banter, but soon realized that Cathy was not responding similarly—something seemed to be bothering her.

He asked her how she had been, and Cathy poured her heart out to him, intermittently punctuated with sobs and sniffs. Chris didn't interrupt her even once. When she had finished, he spoke very slowly and softly, 'Look, my love, things are not going to work out. He is not coming back. The scumbag wanted your money and your body, and now he has got both. There is nothing left for you to offer him anymore, as harsh as it may sound. You need to move on, and this is how you will do it.

'First, move out of Goa and go to Delhi. I am now stationed in Kabul, and I have heard of a university here called the Anglo-American University of Kabul. You can find more details on the net. I am going to try and get you a job. It is the middle of the semester, so you may not find a teaching job, but I think there is an administrative post that is still vacant. But this will take time; it is Kabul after all. A series of background checks will have to be conducted after your interview.

'I will transfer some money into your account; feel free to give it back to me when you start earning it again. I suggest you go to Delhi and stay in a small hotel or an Airbnb, as you will need to make several rounds of the Afghan embassy there.

Let me see how fast I can fix things for you. I just wish you had kept in touch, by now I would have had you here!'

Cathy agreed to what Chris had suggested. The thought of going to Kabul made her nervous, but she saw no other choice. She decided to pack her belongings and wait for Chris's money to come through, and then she would be on a flight to Delhi. She decided not to tell Ian or call him again … or at least try not to.

It took her fifteen days to finish the interview, complete the paperwork and make several rounds of the Afghan embassy. Finally, she got her one-month visitor's visa to Kabul. On a Saturday morning, she took the early morning flight of two hours to Kabul from New Delhi, with her head covered in a scarf just as she had been instructed. She was flying into an alien land, all alone, gripped with apprehension and a feeling of gloom sitting heavily on her chest.

The airport was chaotic, with huge burly men pushing things around. She managed to salvage her only blue suitcase from the carousel with some difficulty.

She was then taken to a dilapidated room where some visa forms needed to be filled. She was balancing her laptop, her purse and her head scarf while she completed the paperwork.

The walk towards the gate with endless street urchins tugging and pulling at her dress while she pushed her rickety trolley while also holding on to her belongings was a difficult job. She managed to smile at those dirty yet cherub-faced little boys and navigated her way.

On her arrival at the gate, she was whisked away in a golden-coloured armoured car, which was not in excellent condition.

She could only catch a few glimpses of a dusty city with half-finished buildings and makeshift carts selling fruits, nuts and some locally made sticky sweets.

The university looked forbidden and unapproachable with its high walls and barbed wire. Several roadblocks that had been placed on the road leading to it gave her the feeling of entering a maze.

There were armed security guards everywhere, dressed in black outfits belonging to a private security group, toying with their AK-47s. She was quickly directed to a shipping container, which was to become her house. In her room, she flopped on to the hard bed. It had been a long journey for her, from England to Iraq to Goa and now Kabul. She sighed and just hoped that she would become a bit wiser and not repeat the foolish mistakes of her past. This time, she was determined to emerge as a winner, determined to do whatever it took to become an achiever.

Nadia

What does an Afghan girl dream of? Are her dreams the same as those of others around the world? Are they allowed to pursue their dreams? Are they free to choose their own path?

These and many such thoughts intrigued Nadia, the daughter of a single mother who worked the whole day to feed Nadia and her three siblings.

Nadia's father was a soldier who had died an untimely death in one of the remotest provinces of Afghanistan. She was barely one year old then and didn't remember him too well, except for the stubble on his cheeks that used to prick her when he used to rub his face on her soft, pudgy one. Madar Jan, as she called her mother, said that after three boys, her father was ecstatic to have a baby girl and would hold her close to his bosom the entire day when he visited them during his annual leave. He just wouldn't let her out of his sight and used to play with her whenever he had some free time; she was his doll. He had promised to bring a beautiful pink frock and toys for his princess the last time he went away, something that he could never do. Madar Jan's eyes became moist every time she spoke about him; she was still so much in love with him.

Marrying another man was not an option for her mother, although there were plenty of them in their Pashtun clan who wanted to accept her and her four kids as their own.

Soon, she got a job on compassionate grounds as a martyred soldier's widow. It was arranged by a friend of her husband, who was the security supervisor at an international university in Kabul.

She was to work in the university canteen, preparing meals or taking orders or at times handling the cash machine. She came from a respectable family and was respected amongst her co-workers.

Half her earnings were spent on educating her children, and she made no difference between her sons and her only daughter, as she knew that this was what her husband desired. All of them should be treated equally and given the same opportunity to flourish in life. The other half of her earnings went to pay for rent, food and clothes for her little ones as they were growing rapidly. Her eldest was now a six-foot-tall lad, just like his father; time was passing so quickly.

Nadia was pampered by her mother and her three elder brothers; they indulged her and catered to her whims and fancies. At times, she behaved very irrationally and was unusually demanding. Like the time when she wanted a pair of jeans and a T-shirt like those that were worn in Bollywood movies. They never said no to her and gave her what she wanted.

Nadia, when she was not being pampered, was an obedient student, diligent in her studies. Her mother was strict with her schooling, and she reciprocated by securing good marks in her exams and was known as one of the brightest in her class, already fluent in Dari, Pashto and English.

When Nadia passed her school with flying colours, her mother took her marks sheet to the president of the university where she worked. As Nadia's mother stood outside the room of this American gentleman, she was visibly nervous, biting her lips and drawing lines on the floor with her toes.

Once called in, she mumbled, 'Sahib, my daughter is very good, she has got good marks, please see her report,' as she held it out for him to see.

'Can you give her admission to the university on a scholarship? I cannot pay her fees, but I am willing to work extra hours for her education.

'She must become independent and start to earn. The future of the women of our country must be bright, unlike what I faced in my youth. She is my only daughter; my sons can fend for themselves. It is the daughter I worry about; without education, she will not have a livelihood. She will be under the thumb of her husband, begging him to part with his money. This is something I don't want my little girl to do.'

The president was a kind and fatherly man; he smiled at her. 'You work in the canteen, aren't you under the supervision of Mr Ahmad?

'I have seen you many times, but didn't have the chance to speak to you. When my secretary told me you wanted to speak to me, I thought of the usual—a raise, a bonus or maybe some other facility. I didn't think you were here to plead for your daughter.

'We must be doing something right, as mothers have started thinking about their daughters' futures. They see that education is the only way to social upliftment. Good! I am very happy that you realized it.

'Deposit a copy of her educational documents and an application with my secretary; she will guide you in writing it. Let me see what I can do for your daughter.'

Nadia's mother left with a smile on her face, hoping that maybe her beautiful daughter would now finally get a chance to make it big in this world. Her mind started sketching dreams that could become true very soon.

The first thing Nadia did after getting admission into the business department was to rush to her eldest brother, knowing that her untimely request would not go down well with her mother.

Her eldest brother, Ajmal, had recently started working in a beverage bottling factory. 'You must get me a leather backpack, a big one with enough space, a pair of good sneakers, a new pair of jeans, preferably a black one, and a couple of tops. You know I like bright lipstick; hence, one or two new shades will be okay. Don't forget to get me a new watch, too; this one is old. I have been wearing it for four years. Can I come with you this Friday for shopping? We can go to the new mall; I have been wanting to visit it; it looks grand.' Nadia was babbling away, excited about her future.

Ajmal smiled at his sister, 'Oh, little one, slow down, your brother is not a business owner but a mere factory worker. Your list is going to cost me a fortune, but I promise I will buy all this for you. Not all in the next month, but slowly, one at a time, every month. I shall keep aside a part of my salary and buy these things as your wish is our command, our princess.'

Nadia didn't like what she was told and left with a pout, muttering 'nobody loves me', which she knew would melt her elder brother's heart. Her brother, though, was well-versed in his sister's ways of manipulation.

Nadia's classes started. She fared well in her foundation courses. She was an intelligent girl. For her, these modules were mere repetitions of what she had studied in high school. Professors started recognizing her diligent work and her participation in the class. Her willingness to help in all departmental events didn't go unnoticed either.

The chair of the department soon offered Nadia a part-time job. She was to work with her at the upcoming marketing fair, where she would contact stall owners and luminaries who would be speaking at the occasion. She was also helping in developing the entrepreneurship club at the university. She got very busy, immersing herself in the project, and was happy to earn fifty dollars as her side income, which she was very possessive about.

She wanted to buy the best with the limited money that was at her disposal. She took her best friend, Breshna, with her on the weekends and roamed about in Majid Mall or City Walk.

Nadia was fussy; if she liked a dress, she found it overpriced; if the price was suitable, then the cut and colour were not to her liking. She secretly wished she could go to India to shop, as she had seen photographs of actresses in film magazines and wanted to buy things that they wore.

When she tried on a new dress, she admired herself in the mirror. She knew she was good-looking, but she wanted Breshna's admiration, 'Do I look good? Just like that heroine in the film the other day? Only her dress was blue, and this useless shop has nothing in blue. Do you have a lighter shade of lipstick? Can I borrow it? The shade I have is not suitable for this dress. Please, just for a day till Ajmal buys a new one for me, please.'

She would fold her hands and draw a crying face, and Breshna had no alternative but to yield, knowing that her best friend was incorrigible with her demands.

Everyone was indulgent towards her—she ruled her world; she was the princess of her world. And out of love, everyone catered to her needs and whims; there was no other way anyone would bear to see tears in those lovely eyes.

She was basking in happiness now that she had her income as a part of the work-study programme and started vying for a permanent job at the university. Her professors were more than happy to give her a recommendation letter. Some even suggested that she should try to get a scholarship and attempt to go to the US to complete her master's degree, a thought that appealed to her.

She took some glossy brochures; they were kept in the library in bunches, and students were picking them up. The brochures were from various universities in the US that were offering partial or full scholarships.

The brochures had pictures of the university halls, the student dormitories, the canteens and the playgrounds. Nadia got lost in those pictures, dreaming of climbing those large steps or playing basketball in the play area. Nadia was very excited because her

GPA score matched their requirements, and she had some excellent recommendation letters and work certificates. There was no holding her back; it was just a matter of time before she would be on an airplane, off to America.

That day, the journey back home to her house in Khair Khana was long. It took her nearly an hour and sometimes more, depending on the traffic. She was restless and fidgety in the shared cab. She clutched the brochures, and when she reached home, she galloped her way to the third floor, missing a few steps each time.

On reaching home and plonking herself on the carpet, she was a bit surprised to see her mother and her elder brother looking sombre, with her aunt sitting next to them.

She tried to lighten the atmosphere by saying, 'Don't waste time, Madar Jan. And you, too, brother, start preparing for my flight to America! I am sure to get my scholarship, and off I go in less than six months.'

Her mother didn't smile and looked at her brother. He asked her to come and sit close to them while her aunt continued sipping tea from her cup. Something had gone wrong; Nadia felt this sense of foreboding. She sat straight, drew her legs closer and pulled her skirt to hide her toes.

Her brother cleared his throat and said, 'Nadia Jaan, you know how much we love you; you mean everything to us. The environment in our country is deteriorating. The Taliban are coming to power, and the US troops are no longer going to be there to protect us. We are hearing of Taliban activities in the Kandahar region. If they get hold of Kabul city, they will drag out every woman of marriageable age and throw them to their soldiers. You are very pretty and noticeable among many. We won't be able to face a calamity like that. And thus, we have decided to get you married.

'Do you remember our tenant from almost ten years ago? Zahirullah, that young lad who enrolled himself in the army? Aunty here has come to speak about your nikah to him. He is from our tribe, known to us, and from a good family. He is the eldest son; you will be happy with him. He will know how to protect and take care of you.'

Nadia couldn't believe what she had just heard; how could her brother and mother be so cruel? She was still pursuing her dreams, holding those colourful brochures of American colleges in her hands. All she wanted was to study, do well in life and not get married to someone she barely remembered. She tried to protest, but her voice gave way. Only tears streamed down her face.

She got up and rushed out, heading straight for her room. She threw herself on her pillow and sobbed uncontrollably for almost an hour, her dreams melting away with her tears, like the kohl of her eyes. Then she got tired and dozed off to sleep, her sneakers still on her feet and the brochures clutched in her hand.

The day of the wedding came soon. Everything had to be rushed, and Nadia barely had any time to comprehend what was happening. She was pulled from one side to the other, selecting her dresses, the makeup, the bangles, the jewellery. She ran to and from the tailor to the salon, and then to the jeweller, and still managed her studies.

She was torn between her ambition to pursue her studies and her duty to be an obedient daughter to her mother and cater to her wishes. Nadia's mother and brothers left no stone unturned to give her a fairy-tale wedding. They borrowed money, reached out to family members for their generous contributions and staged a three-day-long celebration.

Nadia looked like a diva in her red, green and white flowing gowns and jewellery, earmarked for those three days of celebrations. The groom, Zahir, looked handsome in his suit and traditional wear. There were not many chances for them to get to know each other before the wedding, so they occasionally stole shy glances when they were around each other.

Nadia was beginning to think that life was not as bad as she had imagined it to be. Maybe this was for the best; she would now bask in the love of a man to whom she belonged. And if what Ajmal said about the Taliban coming to their city was true, she would still be safe in his arms. Zahir was a fighter and would protect her with all his might, hiding her with his large frame and defending her honour with his strong arms.

After the wedding, she came to stay at Zahir's house. It was a two-storey building with uncemented brick walls that housed him and his extended family. His own family was designated to have two rooms, which they shared. Since they were a newly married couple, they were given a small attic room that hardly had any furniture, but a wall-to-wall, musty, faded carpet.

Nadia was expected to live out of her suitcase and a bag that was pushed to one side of the wall. Much to her dismay, the room had a very small window. This meant the room was dark most of the time, making it difficult for her to read or work on her laptop. One bathroom was shared by twenty-five other members of the family, and waiting for it in line in the morning was no less than an ordeal. She started accepting it as her fate, but what she failed to accept was the ruthlessness of her husband.

First, he made her delete all her social media accounts, saying that they were haram. Then he stopped her from wearing jeans, colouring her nails, cutting her hair, putting on lipstick, wearing perfume, listening to music, watching movies—everything for him was haram. According to him, her prime duty was to bear children as soon as possible.

He was brutal when it came to lovemaking, and every night became a nightmare for her. He twisted her, turned her, mangled her and entered her as many times as he wanted with no regard for her cries or her muffled sobs. Nadia, being an intelligent girl, knew that this ordeal would last every night between eighteen to twenty-five minutes. In those twenty-odd minutes, he was possessed by some kind of rage. As he grabbed and groped her, he would keep mumbling the same words repeatedly, as if in some kind of frenzy, with instructions or a relay of what he was about to do. The trick was to moan and groan loudly under him, and then the ordeal would be shorter—a blessing for Nadia. She woke up with bruises on her back, neck, face and legs, but she was too ashamed to talk about it to anyone.

After a few months, she mustered the courage and spoke to her mother one day. Madar Jan dismissed it as Zahir being a passionate man, appeasing her by ensuring her that these would subside once they had a child. She kept pleading, 'Madar Jan, I cannot be with this man, he will kill me one day. He is brutal; he treats me as his sex slave. Please let me come back and stay with you. I will study hard and get a job and earn enough for all of us. Please, don't discard me; I am your only dokhtar. Please help me.' But her mother was adamant. She was now married and belonged to Zahir; she must have the courage to settle down in a marriage and bear patiently what Allah had ordained for her.

As life went on, Nadia kept suffering. Her health started failing and her education suffered. She still worked at the university as her husband had no job. He waited every month to snatch her salary from her. Resisting him would only mean more punishment and being subjected to worse physical abuse.

The once-delicate flower of a girl, whom everyone doted upon, started withering. One could see the dark circles under her eyes. Her vibrant smile disappeared and her once-glowing skin lost its sheen. She slowly learned to remain silent and accept her fate, yet her mind remained active, thinking every moment of a way to escape this ordeal. She needed to run away or she would soon die. Death would be more welcome than this humiliating life. She was not willing to accept this as her fate, not her.

Anjali

Be a good student at school, go for higher education, then, perhaps, get a job and, ultimately, get married. This is the linear pattern for a girl from a middle-class family in India, with seldom any deviation. Anjali Kumar was no exception; she was a middle-class girl who graduated from Calcutta University, pursued her master's degree and then moved to Delhi to get her doctoral degree.

This was when she got married to Abhay Sharma, an engineer with a good job, who had prospects of moving to the US. Anjali was happy to become Mrs Abhay Sharma and so was her family.

Her mother blessed her, saying, 'Beta, you are so blessed, he is like a prince—so handsome and rich—and he has a bright future ahead of him and you, too, as you complete your studies. What more could a mother want? I am waiting for the day when I will come to the US to help you with the birth of my grandson, a little flower born to the Sharma family and ours. Oh! Such happiness, I am counting the days.'

Everything in their life was planned. The completion of her PhD, his transfer to Chicago, her postdoctoral degree, a cushy lectureship and then starting their family with one or two kids.

There was no scope for speculation, no risk-taking, no maybe, could be, perhaps, in their life. This was how it was going to be—a happy life with the blessings and love of elders, a blossoming romance between the young couple and a dreamy future ahead.

Then, one day, Abhay vomited after having his glass of milk at breakfast. He vomited again after dinner, and he kept vomiting every time a morsel of food entered his stomach. As the day passed, he complained of weakness and a slight fever.

His parents spoke about the viral fever that was becoming quite prevalent among city dwellers. Her parents advised her to give him buttermilk and nothing else; it could be a bad stomach bug that he must have picked up when he ate something outside.

The sisters and brothers had their fair share of advice on boiled water, light toast, soup, staying in bed, covering him with a blanket—an endless list of what should be done, what was not being done and what she had been neglecting.

'Don't let him go out, don't let him get up from his bed, don't let him eat spicy food, nothing from outside at all. Don't give him hot tea, put some salt in his water, he might be dehydrated, the rice should be doubly boiled, massage some hot oil under his feet …'

The list was endless, and so was the advice. Anjali listened to everything and tried all the home remedies, and all kinds of anti-vomiting drugs and paracetamol as advised by a relative who was also a doctor.

But Abhay was just not getting better. He would be okay for an hour or two and then he would relapse. Gradually, his health showed more signs of weakness. He was unable to stomach food or even liquid, and there was swelling in his limbs.

Anjali had this strong premonition that something was seriously wrong somewhere, and it was taking a turn for the worse. Her mind conjured up all sorts of possibilities—and none of them were pleasant.

A consultation with the doctor and a blood test with a waiting period of three days, then a twenty-four-hour urine test confirmed her worst fear: Abhay was losing both his kidneys. The creatinine level would not be repaired with mere tablets and capsules; the couple would have to prepare for his dialysis very soon.

They sat for hours staring blankly at the wall with the diagnosis report in hand, as if a thunderbolt had struck them. Hours of hugging each other and crying did not reverse the situation. Counting the money in their savings account again and again did not reverse the situation. And the siblings making excuses and gradually moving away so that they wouldn't have to contribute also did not reverse the situation.

Anjali and Abhay understood that they should brace themselves for a long battle ahead. This battle would have many hurdles, all to be faced by a young couple who would now have to unlearn to dream.

Abhay kept asking her every day, 'What will happen, Anjali? I don't want to die so young. I have lots to see and do; can you save me, please?'

Anjali kept assuring him, 'I am here with you, don't worry, we will see this through.' She still couldn't remember how she mustered up the courage to say those words of encouragement when she was sinking slowly into the abyss, not being able to find a way out.

Abhay could now eat and drink a limited amount and only a few items. Every sneeze, cough, fever and other symptom had to be reported to the doctor, followed by a series of tests. His daily consumption of medicine exceeded his intake of food; his weight needed to be monitored, as well as his lipids and vitals. Endless visits to doctors and waiting in line for hours for a scan or an X-ray would make the couple exhausted and depressed, yet the battle carried on.

Very soon, Abhay was put on dialysis. Anjali struggled to balance her income, her savings, her job and looking after him.

Anjali and Abhay realized that their life was now very different from others and decided to move to a tiny apartment close to the hospital; they were now on their own.

Anjali prayed every day that she would emerge as a winner from this battle. It was not only Abhay's life, but her own life entwined with his that was at stake too.

Dialysis could not be a long-term solution for someone as young as Abhay. Anjali was asked to arrange for a transplant before his body became too weak to undergo surgery. She sold her last set of ornaments and depended on a donation drive from her colleagues in the new college where she had started teaching. Abhay could raise some money on his own, as he now worked from home as a consultant.

From six in the evening till three in the morning, Anjali stood alone in the cold corridors of the hospital, near the operating theatre. She broke down into loud sobs when the doctor came out and congratulated her that Abhay's transplant had been a success. The three-month quarantine period passed, and Abhay became stronger by the day.

The illness had taken a toll on their financial and mental well-being. Anjali sat on the bed and reached out to touch Abhay's hand, who smiled meekly at her.

'Abhay, how do you feel now? I am glad that you are recovering. I was just sitting and thinking that this had been a very tough journey for both of us. It taught me a lot, but the most important lesson has been that we need to be in good health and have a lot of money. And that we are all alone and friendless in this world. There is no one to help us.'

'What do you have in mind? You are not someone who says things for the sake of uttering them; go on, tell me, what do you have in mind?'

'Yes, you are right, we need to build on two things: our finances and your health, mine too. I saw some jobs in the Middle East for both of us in academia. If we apply, we might get good perks. What do you think?'

'The day I became sick, I realized that I could depend on no one but you. Please do what you think will be best for both of us. I am with you in everything. Do you think I can teach students? If you have the confidence, then I am on board.'

◈

In the next six months, Anjali moved with her husband to Saudi Arabia. The job was good, and the money was even better, and they slowly started rebuilding their finances.

After eight years of working there, Abhay became sick again, and they rushed back to India to seek medical help. And this time, things seemed to be going downhill much faster. Anjali had only one goal in mind: to save Abhay.

They toured the entire country from south to north and west to east, looking for a doctor who would give her husband a new lease of life. And then, one day, after eight months of struggle, Abhay succumbed to surgery in the wee hours of a Friday morning.

Anjali was all alone and had to manage the funeral of his cold, listless body lying on the tray in a morgue. She braced herself and did what was required from a religious point of view. Once again, a dutiful wife, slowly removing all the telltale signs of a married woman that adorned her body. With this, her soul, too, became bare of all colours and emotions.

Anjali lost the purpose of her life. Unable to bear the pain of her loss and the thought of impending loneliness for the rest of her life, she attempted suicide, failed and was hospitalized. She was saved, but she gave up food and even water and, severely dehydrated, she was taken to the hospital bed again.

She was kept on sleeping pills, her heart rhythm slowed down. She was unable to digest even a morsel of food, and was physically and mentally a wreck.

Some days, she would just sit staring at the walls. Sometimes she would wail and cry her heart out, or keep listening to Abhay's voice messages, or just hold his shirt close to her chest. She had this incessant desire to meet him once more, talk to him, sleep beside him, hear him breathe, hold his soft hands and cross the road.

She tried vacations, shopping, meeting friends and reading, but nothing worked; nothing ever did. Then one day, her friend, whom she had met in Saudi Arabia, suggested that she should apply for a job in Kabul as an assistant professor.

Anjali was not very sure whether she would like to take up a job in Kabul. It was not one of the safest places on earth. Things were different now; she was alone, not a married woman with her husband beside her. She had heard stories of abductions and disappearances of single women, and the news coverage also confirmed some of her fears. She kept toying with the idea for some time, and then, when living with Abhay's memories in the house became unbearable, she applied for the job.

After several rounds of interviews, background and police checks, she left her house to reach Kabul, after having packed Abhay's passport in her purse and his blue T-shirt, which he was wearing on the last day, in her suitcase.

She locked the apartment. His slippers were still on the shoe rack, and his towel was folded neatly on a table. The mineral water bottle from which he drank water for the last time was on the bedside table. So were his bottles of pills, his eye drops, his balm for his headaches—everything remained as it was, in its place. Only the two souls in love had departed, one for an alien world and the other for the realm beyond this world. Their smiling faces in the photos kept hanging on the blank wall.

◈

On her last night at home, she listened to songs that he liked, 'Are You Lonesome Tonight', the deep voice of Elvis Presley filling their bedroom. This was his favourite; tears flowed and soaked her pillow.

The next morning, Anjali was up and about cleaning her apartment. Her bags were packed and she was ready to leave for the airport. Leaving all this behind to go to a new land, hoping her heart would heal, if not whole, a little bit.

When she reached Afghanistan, she found solace in the fact that even in this remote corner of Kabul, he was with her. When she went back, walking from the office building to her container, nearly three thousand steps, she became breathless with the thick, dry wind clasping her chest tightly. She felt that he was holding her hand and walking with her, her small fist in his large one so that she didn't miss a step.

Zohra

The summer heat can make dribbling a football difficult. One would be all sweaty and sticky, whether it was a green field in Toronto or a dusty field in Kabul, thought Zohra. Her T-shirt was clinging to her body, her armpits were soaked in sweat and her hair, tied in a knot, had sweat settling in it.

She didn't feel like fishing for her headscarf in her backpack and tying it around her sweaty hair and neck. One day without a headscarf wouldn't bring the heavens down on her, she smiled mischievously as she thought to herself.

She pulled the bag, slinging it across her shoulder, and headed towards her apartment, a huge apartment complex that housed many Afghan families who had come to Canada in the 1990s as refugees.

Zohra hardly had any memory of Kabul apart from the occasional visits to her grandmother's place when she was very young. Those visits stopped after her demise. Her father loved traveling and took them to various places in the US or Europe instead of reconnecting with his large and extended family back home in Afghanistan. She only saw her relatives when someone came from Kabul for a visit, a medical emergency or for admitting their sons and daughters in educational institutions in Canada.

As Zohra marched on, she knew her clinging, damp T-shirt drew disapproving glances from the aunts who were standing downstairs, basking in the summer sun. Zohra knew that this would be their dining-table talk for today, and she giggled, thinking about how they would hem and haw.

'Allah! Khan Sahib's daughter is a complete rogue. Fatima is not doing a good job of bringing up this girl. Did you see how she was dressed? Couldn't she put a scarf on her head? Surely, she realizes that she is not a young child anymore. Mark my words, very soon she will run away with some white boy. They will regret that they have given so much freedom to an Afghan girl.'

'Why? Why does she need to play football? Is she a boy? Huh? Can't she learn to cook and stitch at this time? Alas! I wish we were in our Watan, our land, and then we could have brought up these girls according to our culture.'

The aunts would gossip some more and then move on with their litany of complaints: moan and groan about the weather, how the food was so tasteless, how they missed the berries and the peaches. Why couldn't they make a perfect bolani in this blessed land? The list was endless. The narrative was always the same. Zohra had a good idea of penning their woes someday and distributing a booklet titled: '100 reasons for an Afghan mother to complain'.

The story was the same in her house, too. As soon as her mother set her eyes on her, she started screaming in her shrill voice.

'Zohra, my God! Don't you have any shame, galloping up the stairs like a horse in a clingy T-shirt? Don't you have a headscarf in your bag? Couldn't you have wrapped it around?

'Shameless girl! How many times do I have to teach you? What do you want, huh? What do you want? That white boys look at your body lecherously or drag you to some corner, is this what you want?

'You are going to bring shame to your father and our family. Do you think you are still a baby, huh? Go stand in front of the mirror and look at yourself. For heaven's sake, look at your T-shirt, it is like wearing next to nothing, Ya Allah!'

'Mumsie, I am sweating. It is hot, I am sticky and dirty. Let me have a bath, and I shall listen to all your complaints. Please, not now.'

Fatima sat down on the sofa and nodded her head gravely. This did not look good. It was taking a wrong turn, and she was scared that it might escalate. This daughter of hers was becoming a rebel, so she decided to discuss it with her husband at night.

Her daughter refused to listen to her nowadays. Soon, it would be difficult to find a groom for her, and what if anything unpleasant happened? Then they would never be able to show their face to society anymore. Their pride and prestige would be smeared with shame.

She must and she should discuss this with her husband tonight itself, and find a solution. She would urge him to work on this as his priority, finding an appropriate groom and getting Zohra married as soon as possible.

Zohra was an average student but was very good at sports. Her coach was impressed with her performance and decided to call her and tell her that she could apply for a scholarship to study at any of the prestigious universities in Canada or the US based on her achievements in sports. She was also told that a career in the army was a good option for her.

She was excited and decided to discuss it with her parents, sometime very soon, when the thought of her exams, overall scores and rank was out of their heads.

Also, they were busy preparing for the upcoming Eid celebration as they had decided to invite all their cousins who were settled in Canada. The house was being scrubbed and polished, and pickles and sweets were being tried out every day in the kitchen. Now was not a suitable time for such discussions; it needed to be shelved for a couple of weeks.

Eid had always been special in this family. Zohra's father wanted to relive the moments of the Eid celebration in Kabul. He wanted the best to be served, the best to be eaten and the best to be gifted. No one could argue with him. Finally, the special day arrived, and the aroma of Kabuli pulao, the smell of nutmeg and saffron from the meat curry, along with the freshly baked pineapple cake, wafted in the air and lingered in each room.

The tables looked colourful with lollipops made from fresh fruits. The pudding was garnished with pomegranate, and freshly squeezed fruit juices were placed in jars. Children were running around, nibbling the food and creating messes everywhere. Cleaning after Eid was always a chore.

Men were confined to one room, sipping green tea with roasted pistachios and almonds. They were discussing the same old topic of how cheap dry fruits used to be back at home and how the prices here were skyrocketing. The topic soon turned to politics: how the condition in Kabul was rapidly changing and who could be the next president.

Zohra was called to the room where her aunts were sitting. Her mother ordered her to sit with them instead of looking for a pretext to go out and spend time with her friends. The air in the room was heavy with the smell of perfume and new clothes, as they shifted onto the sofa or the bed. One could hear the rustling and crackling of silk garments and the fake gilded work on them.

Today was one of those days she didn't ignore her mother's command. She sat down as an obedient, dutiful daughter, sipping some pomegranate juice from a glass. The admiring glances of her aunts surprised her. They praised her thick hair, long, tapered fingers and light-green eyes. They commented about her healthy, fair complexion and her red lips, which appeared redder after gulping down a glass of pomegranate juice.

Zohra kept wondering what all this fuss was about. Everyone, including the uncles, had been especially nice to her, looked at her kindly and spoke to her in a caring and loving tone. Maybe they had come to know that next Eid she would perhaps be in another city, another university or maybe another country.

After two days of celebration, everyone left one by one, leaving the house to be cleaned and arranged by them. Both mother and daughter got busy with it with little or no help from the men in the house. Zohra resumed her classes and got busy practicing for the upcoming football match.

◈

One evening, her parents called her to their room.

'Dokhtar Jaan, you know we love you a lot. It is time that we start thinking about your marriage.'

'Mother, come on, I have barely completed my bachelor's degree. I am more bothered about my master's and getting a good job; marriage is the last thing on my mind.'

'It might be the last thing on your mind, but it is the first thing we think about when we get up in the morning; we cannot avoid our responsibilities or even forget about our culture. As a good Afghan daughter, you will do what we want you to do.' The last bit was added by her father in a very strict tone.

They proceeded to describe a prospective groom who was distantly related to them and who had just secured a good position in the Da Bank, which was the central bank in Afghanistan. He was a good, sensitive young man who was well-educated and had a good prospect in the organization where he was working.

He had a younger brother and two sisters who were studying. Along with his parents, they stayed near Shar-e-Naw, in one of the posh localities in Kabul. The marriage would be online, sanctified in the presence of a moulavi from both sides. Zohra would fly to Kabul to start staying with her husband and his family.

'Online marriage, like a Zoom call or a Google Meet? Really? Are you kidding me? And I don't get to see this "good groom"?

Talk to him or even find out how tall he is, or what his likes and dislikes are? Do they even match mine? This is what you have planned for my future, I am so amused!'

'Stop being sarcastic with your parents. Yes, this is what we have planned and this is what we will do. Our culture is not going to discotheques with your future husband or a resort before marriage,' her mother responded.

She continued, 'You are of marriageable age. After this, no Afghan boy will marry you. And if they get to hear that you have several white male friends, they will not even look at you. Then what will you do? Remain a spinster for the rest of your life, or get a Canadian to marry you in a church, huh?'

Zohra tried to protest, 'But Mom, Dad, you came to this country, you gave me a good education. A lifestyle that I am used to—and it doesn't match the one in Kabul. A holiday is fine, but a lifelong marriage? How am I going to adjust? I can barely speak properly in Pashto.'

Fatima hardened her jaw, 'You will learn. We all did. The journey from Kandahar to Kabul and then to Canada when I was barely in my twenties was not easy. We all learn. We have our husband and family by our side; what more can we ask for? You, too, will learn.'

A month-long negotiation, crying, emotional blackmail, fasting, sulking or even threats to run away didn't have any effect on her parents. She was dolled up and was made to sit in front of the computer while her parents and relatives kept beaming in the background.

She saw her husband for the first time. She had no choice but to nod her head in affirmation when Moulavi Saab asked her whether she agreed to marry him.

The next day, Zohra was on a long journey to Kabul, which required her to change three flights. As the flight took off, she leaned on the window, tears trickling down her face.

◈

In Kabul, Zohra met her husband for the first time. He was a kind and timid man who barely had a voice of his own, but her mother-in-law was just the opposite.

To her, Canada-born Zohra was useless—not good at cooking, not aware of her culture and someone who didn't know how to respect elders. Her sole aim was to look for pretexts to humiliate Zohra. If that could be done in front of a room full of people, then her joy knew no bounds.

Three months into the marriage, Zohra realized that her only way of dealing with this was to stay away from the house for as long as possible. She had heard of the international university and thought that her escape would come in the form of a job in the administrative department at the university. She was a smart girl, and after a round of interviews and a written test, the job was hers.

Her mother-in-law agreed because some extra money would flow into the family account and then they could add another storey to their existing house. Zohra kept gritting her teeth and counting every passing day, waiting to get the next opportunity to go back to Canada. She was regularly in touch with her friends and her teachers, who promised her a bright future at a university for her to pursue her master's degree.

She started liking her timid husband and secretly wished that he, too, could accompany her if they got the opportunity to go back, away from her tyrant mother-in-law.

In moments of tenderness, she would nestle close to his chest, whisper words of endearment and slowly push her agenda to go back. Yes, she knew she was manipulating him, but there was no other way.

Her husband would listen to her, his voice thick with passion, and mumble, 'Is this what you want? Do you think it will be good for us? But my mother …' She would place her lips on his and silence him. And he, lost in her soft folds, would succumb to anything that she was plotting and hatching in her mind.

Fawzia

Fawzia woke up with a heavy heart. A sense of drudgery seemed to have flowed through her body during the night, making her limbs heavy and her head throb with a dull pain.

Recently, these feelings seemed to have become a common phenomenon; she hated waking up. She hated opening her eyes to the world around her. She secretly wished that she could sleep forever and not wake up from her deep slumber.

A sense of foreboding gripped her chest. She felt an immense fear that was almost paralysing. She shouldn't indulge in listening to the radio or her neighbours. They were all talking about the old Talib regime coming back soon; that they had occupied half of the provinces already. Very soon, they would be in Kabul; they seemed to have captured Kandahar and were moving towards Nimroz province. Reaching the gates of Kabul was only a matter of time.

Fawzia was filled with dread. How was she going to work and feed her son? She would be flogged and kicked out on the road, maybe even stoned to death.

She vaguely remembered how life had been in her childhood some twenty, twenty-five years back, when she was barely eight years old. She and her siblings used to huddle under blue burqas and go out only occasionally with their father or their uncle accompanying them. There were no schools for them, only what her father taught her at home—to read the holy Quran and sign her name.

No. She shook her head, she shouldn't think of such things early in the morning. She reached out for her crutch from the bedside and stood up with a moan. The leg still hurt and so did her backbone.

She dragged herself out of bed; there was too much to do. These days, they were getting electricity supply only for an hour in the morning and an hour in the evening in Kabul.

There was a lot to do at home before she went to the university. She must fill up all the buckets, pots and pans, and prepare all the meals for the day. She called out to her son softly to wake him up. He looked like an angel sleeping on his bed near hers. He was the only good thing that had happened in her marriage. The rest was all a disaster, a traumatic past.

She knew her pain was lifelong. She was caged in it, and there was no escaping it. Her only hope was her son, who was an intelligent boy of eight. Perhaps, he would someday become a big officer and provide a comfortable life for his mother. She smiled, dreaming of a bright future with her son. This motivated her to push herself a little more, to do some more work and earn a decent living to support both of them.

Fawzia was so ordinary that you would miss her if she were in a crowd. Nothing was striking about this Hazara woman, except when she smiled; her bright smile lit up her entire face. It was with her smile that Ali, her neighbour, fell in love with as he would see her walking past his house, chatting with her friends and smiling on her way to the bazaar every Friday.

She was a good cook; her mother had taught her well. She would cook for her entire household on Fridays. That day, her parents decided to take some rest.

She liked hand-picking fresh ingredients from the bazaar.

She would pick a bunch of coriander and smell them. She would hold the tomatoes in her hand and squeeze them to check their ripeness. She rubbed the onions on her scarf to reveal their pinkish hue, or the carrots to display their bright orange colour. She pricked the lemon with her finger for the tangy aroma to spread on her fingers and all around her.

The vegetable seller would gently scold her, 'Fawzia Jan, I don't have all the time in this world for you; there are other customers lined up behind you. Stop playing with the vegetables, will you?'

Fawzia would smile at Haji Uncle, the vegetable seller who had seen her from her childhood, and hurried to put the vegetables in her bag. There was much to do at home. She had to clean, cut and cook these vegetables as a delicacy. She was mentally working on the menu. Would it be bolani or just plain vegetables with tomatoes and a handful of nice pink lentils thrown in?

She would pick a piece of juicy mutton rib on her way home, there was enough money for that, too. Chop, slosh, sizzle, these were her favourite sounds. Music to her ears whenever she cooked. She liked to see the colours changing and the softness of the vegetables as they were sautéed and fried. The aroma—mainly the aroma—she wished she could bottle them and keep them as perfumes on her tiny dressing table. Her perfect life, her kitchen on Fridays, her loving family and her corner in the house, life for her was a fairy tale. She often reminisced about those days, now nine years in the past, when she was unmarried and still stayed with her parents in their house. It was the last Eid before her marriage …

Eid was just around the corner. Fawzia had to prepare sweets for everyone. She was happy doing so, decorating them with dried fruits and wrapping them in small boxes. Madar Jan was tired due to the preparations for the festival, and Fawzia was asked to distribute the sweets to the neighbours.

She was dressed in a bright pink dress and had touched up her lips with her much-used lipstick. Pulling her scarf on her head, she started floating through the numerous staircases that coiled in front of their house on a mountaintop.

The steps were a bit slippery, but Fawzia was floating; she didn't mind the steps. Suddenly, a shadow blocked her path. It was Ali. He tried to show off his blue sunshades, putting them on his eyes and the next moment putting them on his head. Fawzia tried to move aside without engaging in any kind of conversation.

'Wait, why are you in such a tearing hurry all the time? I have been trying to talk to you for several days and you don't even notice. Why?'

She was a bit taken aback. So far, no boy had attempted to speak to her. She got flustered and looked up. Ali was taller than her, and she squinted her eyes at the sun's rays.

'Oh! I am sorry, I never realized, did you have some work, did your mother call me?' Ali moved an inch closer to her. She could feel his breath on her cheeks, and that made her very uncomfortable. She blushed. He spoke in a very tender voice, 'You need not be sorry, why should you be?'

He looked directly into her eyes and spoke with a determination in his voice that scared Fawzia. 'I like you; I want you to be my wife.'

'Tauba, I cannot discuss such things. Astaghfirullah! Whatever you need to say, please talk to my father or my elder brother,' saying this, she started climbing down the stairs quickly, her cheeks still burning with shame.

'Wait, don't just walk away. My father will speak to yours. I just wanted to know, do you like me? Tell me that before you run away!'

'I don't know …' her voice trailed away as she reached the bottom of the hill, panting, her chest heaving up and down like a bellow used in an iron shop. Her throat was parched and her hand was trembling. She feared that the neighbours might have seen them together and overheard the conversation. Shameless boy, that Ali. She should try and avoid him from now on; he was nothing but trouble.

She soon forgot about Ali. One afternoon while she was kneading the dough, her mother came hurriedly and told her to wash her hands.

'Do it now, Fawzia Jan! The bread can wait! Wash your face with a bit of soap. Wear that nice pink dress of yours, quickly! Go, my child, go.'

There was urgency and a tearing hurry in her mother's voice. 'Why, Madar Jan, where am I supposed to go now? There is so much to do in the kitchen!'

'Ah! Don't argue with me, my child. Ali and his family have come to ask for your hand in marriage. Allah has blessed us; what more could a mother want? Her daughter is to be married to a healthy, handsome boy, and then live near her even after marriage. That boy has come to be such a good-looking man. He works in a carpenter's shop, he is learning the trade, they say.'

Fawzia's heart leaped to her mouth; she tried to say something to her mother, but she couldn't find the appropriate words. She was in a stupor, standing like a statue in the kitchen. Her mother pushed her out of the kitchen and urged her to get dressed and take the tea to the sitting room, where all had gathered. She did as she was told, and she did what she was not told to do: paint her lips pink, put kohl in her eyes and tie her hair with that shiny band she had bought on Eid.

She liked what she saw in the mirror and blushed secretly. For the first time, she was dressing up to please a man, and this effort was worth it when she saw the admiration in Ali's eyes. She carried the tray of tea and cashew nuts to the room where he was sitting beside his father. The meher (the sum to be paid to the bride) was decided and so was the date of the nikah (marriage).

The days of preparation passed in a daze. The house was filled with the chatter of aunts and uncles and the crying of cousins or the fighting of the younger siblings.

Her hair was oiled and combed several times. Nice-smelling soap was given to her to scrub her body. A paste was made with milk and gram flour to scrub her face. Innumerable pieces of advice were given by elders as to how to behave in the new household and with her husband. She went around nodding her head in agreement with all that was explained and all that remained unexplained but was merely suggested with a wink and a sly smile. Some she understood, some she didn't, but she never bothered to ask anyone.

The wedding took place and she became part of a new family. Her in-laws were happy; they adored her for being a good cook and a quiet little mouse.

She was happy … very happy, as she melted in Ali's arms and he ignited tiny little fires on her fingers, her lips, her eyebrows and the nape of her neck with his passionate kisses. She would do anything to see admiration in his brown eyes. Her world revolved around him. Soon, they welcomed little Arzoo, who played in his parents' lap throughout the day as they took turns cuddling and cooing to him.

◈

Once again, Eid came and the hustle and bustle started in both households. She was running around helping her mother as well as her mother-in-law. Demands were pouring in to cook certain delicacies, and she was scuttling around like a mouse, fulfilling them.

Fawzia remembered that day vividly. She remembered her mother-in-law calling her to her room.

'Make that famous dessert of yours. Now, take some money and get some dry fruits and saffron to put in the dessert. My brother's family is coming. They are visiting after two years from Pakistan. I want to give him the best. Besides, they haven't met you, they couldn't come to the wedding. They will be happy to have something cooked by you.'

It was only eleven in the morning. She had plenty of time to rustle up the dessert and make some fried savouries. She took the bag from the trunk and, folding some money in her handkerchief, she went happily down the stairs.

As she was about to cross the road in front of her when there was a loud, deafening noise, and then everything went black in front of her eyes. All she could feel was something oozing out of her legs and the whole world spinning.

She was told that she was in the hospital for eleven days, drifting in and out of a coma. Her limbs felt as if they were on fire, and the fire was slowly engulfing her, limb by limb. The excruciating pain travelled up to her head. She could barely focus with her throbbing headache, and her eyesight was blurred. She lay lifeless on the hospital bed, tears trickling down from her eyes.

The moment she came into consciousness, she asked for Ali and Arzoo, but her parents avoided the topic.

Days turned to nights and nights to mornings in the hospital. She was given injections and medicines every day to numb her pain and lull her to sleep. Then, one day, she slowly sat up, ignoring her pain. It was then that she realized that she had lost one of her legs in a car bomb blast. Her spinal cord had been injured, and the doctors attending her were of the opinion that she might not be able to walk for the rest of her life.

She howled and cried the whole day, begging everyone in sight to bring Ali to her, but no one listened. Months passed, and she could eventually hobble around on her crutches; the amputated leg had started healing. The doctors promised that soon they would get her a prosthetic one.

Then one day, after much begging and crying, Ali came with Arzoo to meet her. He was not smiling at all.

'I am sorry, I couldn't come. I have a lot of work to do,' he talked to her in a stilted way. 'No, please don't get up from bed. I can't take you home. I cannot take care of you anymore. I don't know how to take care of a crippled woman for the rest of my life. What use will you be?

'I cannot bear to have a woman shifting around in my bed, limbless. You must stay with your parents. This is for the best. Arzoo can stay with you, too.'

Fawzia started feeling dizzy listening to her husband say these words.

'I am thinking of going to Dubai to earn money. I am not sure whether I will meet you before I go.' She saw something in his eyes that day; something she had never anticipated seeing in her beloved husband's eyes. She saw disgust towards her, and she knew right then that it was all over.

His voice continued echoing in her ears long after he had left. Her mind was blank, still trying to comprehend his words. He had kept scrunching his nose and scowling at her. He barely sat on the bed and touched her hand gingerly as if she were a leprosy patient.

After forty days, the hospital discharged her, and she finally came home in her wheelchair. They needed two men to haul her up. Life started again with one leg, no husband, painkillers and a little Arzoo. The NGO gave her a crutch and then an artificial limb; they also got her a job as a helper at the canteen at the university.

She couldn't climb the steps anymore and moved to a tiny new room at the foothill. Her father rented it for her as they would not accept a single woman as their tenant.

A year passed, and then Ali came to visit his parents for fifteen days. He met Arzoo and told Fawzia that he had married a Thai woman in the hotel where he worked, and that she was pregnant with their child. Fawzia heard everything, nodded her head and went to make a cup of tea for him with her famous bolani.

As he left, Fawzia knew the kind of life she had ahead of her. She limped and walked with the help of a prosthetic leg. She had to pay for her treatment, her rent, Arzoo's school fees, cook and clean all by herself. She didn't have the time to think about how her youth was slipping away. Her hands were becoming coarse. Her hair had a few grey strands now and the corners of her mouth drooped.

She needed to carry on for the sake of Arzoo. After all, nothing compels a mother more than the desire to protect and to ensure that her child has the best life that can be given.

Part II

AMADAGI GRIFTAN: TO PREPARE

1

Anjali stood near the parking bay, waiting for Dr Cathy to arrive and looking at the rays of sun reflecting on the bonnets of the parked cars. She felt hesitant and apprehensive. A day trip outside the campus: was it a good idea when the situation was pretty tense outside? Her chain of thought was interrupted as she saw Cathy walking towards her. Anjali didn't have the heart to refuse her offer of going to Hotel Arina. It was not only Cathy's insistence; she, too, was curious to see the world outside the university walls.

The morning hadn't started on a good note. There were no cars booked for them. Cathy shook her head and addressed Lutfi, the radio operator, 'I have given a written requisition for a car and a guard. I even spoke to Braddy, our security director. Please check with him. We have to come back by the afternoon. Why isn't the car ready?'

Before Lutfi could call, Braddy came to meet them. 'Cathy, do you need to go? Is it urgent? I mean, things are not very good outside. Kabul is still safe, but problems are happening in other provinces. Internally displaced people are flocking to Kabul.'

'Why, things look quite peaceful. What's wrong? No gunshots or missiles can be heard!'

'It looks apparently peaceful, but it is not. I am in touch with several security agencies. Just a week back, on 3 August, thirteen people were killed in an Inghimasi or suicide-style operation carried out by the Taliban's "Martyrdom Battalion" aimed at killing the defence minister. He luckily survived. Three days after that, Jowzjan province was captured, and now it is Nimroz. Pictures are being circulated that the Taliban fighters were seen driving and sitting on top of captured military Humvees. They have been seen on luxury SUVs and pickup trucks plying through the streets, holding on to the flying Taliban flags. They have the support of the residents—mostly young men—who cheer them on. It may look peaceful in Kabul, but the reality is different.'

'Don't worry so much, Braddy, my dear. We will not be gone for long, and besides, we will only go to Hotel Arina; it is very safe. Dr Anjali has not seen the city. At least she will see a part of it. Let's go, let us not waste time.'

Anjali sat beside the window. She was curious to see the city. They passed a roadside bazaar. Yellow and white taxis were lined up. As it was the peak of summer, there were small carts selling fruit juices, carrots and oranges. Plastic hair clips, colourful scarves and shimmering dresses for little girls were being sold in roadside stalls. The city looked as it would on any busy day.

There was a long line outside a building. Driver Rahim explained that people were lining up at the ATM to withdraw money, apprehensive that banks might collapse, and they would not have any access to cash.

'ATMs are only allowing people to draw the equivalent of two hundred dollars. People are going to several ATMs and drawing money. We will keep it in the house so that we can access cash. We are also buying rice, wheat and other essentials, and hence their prices have gone up. Who knows what is going to happen? Maybe it's nothing, everyone is panicking for no reason.'

Very soon, they reached Wazir Akbar Khan near the Arg. Rahim explained that Zarnegar Park was nearby, and it looked beautiful in spring. The car turned towards Froshgah Street, and Anjali could see the huge anti-blast walls surrounding the hotel. It looked unwelcoming with tall grey walls and uniformed security personnel with AK-47s in their hands. Once again, doubt crept into her stomach. Maybe it was not such a great idea to come here. As she entered the hotel, her thoughts changed. The hotel was breathtaking, with its white and golden floor. The waiting area was upholstered in warm maroon and yellow and the beautiful paintings and wall hangings spoke of good taste.

It seemed Dr Cathy had been here before. She greeted the young man at the reception and smiled at several others. Soon, they moved to the salon. The Tajik girl who introduced herself as Munira was quick with her scissors. In some time, both the ladies emerged from the salon feeling refreshed and relaxed after a massage and a haircut.

It was almost two in the afternoon. Cathy decided to eat something from a local store and not have the usual coffee and croissants from the hotel. Rahim didn't want them to go to any public restaurant, so he ran across the street and bought hot bolanis wrapped in newspapers. As they sat munching the giant samosas filled with mashed potatoes, Anjali remarked, 'Dr Cathy, do you think the university is overreacting with this whole evacuation plan? The street looks like any street in old Delhi or Hyderabad on a hot summer afternoon. The same kind of fruit vendors, juice stalls, food being fried on the roadside, families out on the street, trying out delicacies … I don't sense any danger or threat!'

Cathy, wiping the oil from her fingers with a tissue, remarked, 'I just hope they are exaggerating and soon we might find out that it is life as usual for us and for the people in Kabul. Nothing changes, and I will only be glad. I hope I was able to show you at least some parts of the city today. Although there is a lot to see and experience, unfortunately, we have borrowed the car only for three hours, and we must go back to the campus.'

The ride back to the campus was a quiet one. As they neared the gate once again, they were burdened with the thought—what next? What was going to happen to them? Anjali thanked Cathy for a wonderful afternoon outside the campus, especially for the delicious bolani. Cathy squeezed her hand and said, 'I, too, enjoyed your company. It was very refreshing to be away from these high, foreboding walls. If we stay here, we will continue to explore the city together. I will meet you tomorrow. Have a restful evening.'

As the evening descended on the campus, Cathy and the others got busy trying to plan for their journey back home, following the instructions of the leadership team.

'Login error, please check your connection.'

'Error 505, please check your connection!'

Every time Cathy attempted to log in to the travel booking portal, these messages flashed on her screen. It had been half an hour, and the air conditioner was failing in this heat. There was no maintenance team on campus as almost all of them had gone back to their villages, sensing the impending trouble.

She coiled her hair up and fixed it with a rubber band, went to the washroom and splashed water on her face and neck. She came back to try with renewed fervour.

Ah! The page finally opened. She moved on from 'manage my booking' to 'select a date' and there it was—'no flights available'. How could that be? She tried again, impatiently scratching her head with the back of a pen lying on the table.

She selected another date. She preferred to fly from Turkey and went directly to the portal of the airline. No flights again. Now, panic started gripping her. She felt a dull pain in her stomach and a lump in her throat. Something was just not right.

She tried from a different sector in the Middle East and murmured to herself, 'Where are you, where is the official carrier of this country? Why is it not showing, why?'

An airline she never wanted to use and about which she had heard horrific stories was the only one showing on her screen. Left with no alternative, she selected a date and the sector. She had no options; she must get out.

She started filling in the details when they had a power cut, and the whole room plunged into darkness. The blue light from the computer made the place look eerie. Ten and then fifteen minutes passed, when the light flickered once, then twice and finally came back. The internet connection took another couple of minutes. She logged in again and the flight was scheduled to leave seven days later, on the seventeenth of this month.

Cathy would have liked to stay till the end of the month, receive her salary and then leave, but Dr Watson urged her to get the tickets as soon as possible. A part of her was still uneasy. Was it the right thing to do, spending so much money? What if it got wasted? What if all this was just panic created for nothing? What if she was the only one stupid enough to run away? Her financial situation was not good, and wastage was not an option now.

She got up, wore a proper shirt over her trousers and decided to go for a walk. A gush of hot air hit her face as soon as she opened the door.

Slowly, she started walking in a contemplative mood, head down, twirling the key chain in her finger, eyes fixed on the pavement. She didn't realize that her walk took her to Dr Watson's building. After a moment of hesitation, she decided to go up to his apartment and knock on the door. The leadership team was housed in a proper building on campus.

Dr Watson opened the door, dressed in casual clothes. Initially, he frowned a bit and then broke into a smile. 'Come in, Cathy, just the right moment. Laura is frying some chicken nuggets to go with the drink. Have a seat, pull over the chair.'

'I am sorry, I hope I didn't disturb you. I was a bit stressed and came out for a walk. Then, I realized I was at your doorstep. I decided to check on you. I just got my tickets. It was very expensive. I couldn't get anything but that budget aircraft to the Middle East. Not to Turkey, of course, which I would have preferred.'

'Sit, sit, I am so glad that you got one. Never mind about the cost. We will look into it, which date is it?'

'Seventeenth, sir.'

'I think that should be good. We can continue the classes till the fifteenth. Speak to the security to arrange a car for you. Check whether someone else is taking the same flight, so that you can have company on the way to the airport. Also, check on Dr Sharma; we need to drop her at her embassy. The Indian government does a good job with evacuation, but it will be only for Indians, I guess.'

Cathy sat with him for another half an hour, enjoying some delicious chicken nuggets. They were discussing the possibilities of the university being operational, online courses and relocation. Everything was still in the air; no concrete plans had been made. No one knew what and how things would unfold. They were happy living in the present, considering it a blessing. They could still sit and chat, eat some good food, sip some wine and discuss politics. Would it last? It was a pertinent question that was lurking in everyone's mind.

They bade each other good night, and Cathy walked back slowly to her room.

She was about to put the key inside her lock when she heard hurried footsteps behind her. She froze. Who could it be at this time?

She only started breathing when she saw Nadia standing beside her and panting.

'What are you doing here at this hour? It's a Friday. Why didn't you go back home? Things are not good in the city. Is your husband coming to pick you up?

'Ma'am, Dr Heather told me to come. I had to copy all her material onto a hard disk and enter some data manually for her research. It was a lot of work and she paid me fifty dollars for it. My husband will be here soon to pick me up.'

'Okay, come in, sit for a while. Here, have a glass of water, do you want some tea or a biscuit?'

'No, ma'am, you are so kind.'

Nadia looked at Cathy with apprehension and then said, 'Ma'am, can I ask you for a favour?'

'Yes.'

'Can I keep this backpack at your place? Let me show you what's inside—some of my clothes, some toiletries, my purse with a few hundred dollars and my passport.' She opened her bag and rifled through everything to show Cathy.

'Ma'am, please. I need to escape with you, whenever you leave. I need to run away or else I will die!'

'What is all this about, Nadia?'

'Ma'am, I cannot live with my husband anymore. He is brutal. He treats me as his slave. He makes me do very bad things.'

They spoke for some time and Cathy patiently listened to this young girl. Nadia left for home a lot calmer than before, her backpack lying in one corner of Cathy's room.

Cathy looked at the old, crumpled canvas bag that was lying so miserably against her wall. She felt that maybe every night, Nadia also hid in a corner, her back towards the wall, just like this bag, trying to hide from her husband. She felt sorry for that young girl. So much to bear at such a young age. Once vibrant,

Nadia was a mere shadow of her former self. If only she could help her. But she couldn't figure out how as yet.

◈

The next morning, an email summoned everyone to the boardroom after lunch. All classes scheduled at that hour were cancelled. Anjali read the email twice. It seemed her class was cancelled too, and that was the only one she had today. Mr Jalaluddin Azmi, the chair of social studies, would present his analysis of the current situation and brief them about the impending trouble.

Anjali had been trying her best to like this colleague of hers since the day she arrived and met him in the office. He was slightly arrogant and conceited; narcissism was written all over his bearded face. He towered at six feet three inches. As he stooped down to talk to his colleagues, it seemed that he also looked down upon them. He had a gruff look, with droopy eyes and a large, squarish face with a mole near his eye. All in all, he had a very formidable look about him. Although, to be fair, he had always been polite and friendly with her.

Still, Anjali felt scared of him. Sometimes she tried to figure out what it was about him that made her nervous.

Lost in her thoughts, she reached the boardroom and saw that nobody was smiling. People were talking to each other in grim tones and there was a sense of foreboding in the room. Everyone seemed to be lost in their thoughts about whether they could go home safely and yet keep their job. Finding a job in the middle of the semester was next to impossible.

Mr Azmi seemed to be staring at Anjali, and when their eyes met, he smiled and nodded at her. She smiled at him, too, although the feeling of discomfort crept up once again. Dr Watson spoke briefly, repeating what he had said the other day when he had called them individually to his room; there was no new information.

Mr Azmi was next to speak. He went on and on talking about different provinces, the people, the culture and the Taliban occupation in the nineties. He spoke about the intervention of the United States and the withdrawal of the troops. It was a long, boring session loaded with data. Anjali couldn't figure out what he was hinting at or the point he was driving at; all she felt was that this man liked to hear his own voice. She kept wondering why this history—or maybe political science—lesson was necessary at this juncture. She was not alone. The boring session came to an end, and everyone was left wondering why this was called in the first place. Everyone had hoped for some new information, new directions or a course of action, but none was provided at that meeting.

Anjali was walking down the stairs when Mr Azmi caught up with her. She was startled but managed to mumble 'Hello, Mr Azmi …'

'You can call me Jalal, ma'am. How are you holding up? Are you going back to India? I love your country. I went to Mumbai for my US visa, had a dosa for the first time and simply loved it!'

He looked at her, 'Whenever I look at you, I see a woman of courage and strength, a real *sherni* (lioness), and you are so gorgeous, too. Don't worry about the impending trouble, all that you are hearing. If you can't go back home, you can stay at my place, for as long as you want.'

Anjali now stopped and turned around in irritation.

'Thank you, Mr Jalal, I am sure my embassy will help. I am in touch with them on a daily basis. We have a common WhatsApp group, you see. I must thank you and your wife for such a noble and generous thought. I am truly overwhelmed.'

'I am not married, Dr Anjali,' he added with a chuckle. 'I stay with my brothers. I have my sisters-in-law and enough kids at home; you might like being there with us. It's kind of a full house with ample hustle and bustle. I can give my room to you. It's in the attic, very quiet, and with pleasant scenery around it. It's on a highway going towards the south of the country.'

'That's indeed a lovely description, very suitable for a house-on-the-hire kind of advertisement. If it is needed, I will surely consider your generous offer.'

'I often think about you. On the days that I don't see you or talk to you, I feel something is missing. I don't have too many friends here. Just another colleague of mine—you know him—and maybe you, if I can add you to the list.'

By now, Anjali wanted to move away from where this conversation was going.

But he continued, 'You need to exercise; you are getting out of breath. I bought a yoga mat, which was difficult to find in Kabul, and I had to do quite a bit of searching. Maybe you can exercise for ten minutes a day. You need to be strong, like a lioness, made of steel. Sorry, I am being garrulous. I get nervous talking to you, sorry.'

He kept walking with Anjali towards her room, talking about his mother, his brothers and his childhood. All along, Anjali kept thinking about what this man wanted from her. Why was he trying to be so friendly, polite and helpful? That too, only when they were about to leave the campus. Surely, he had an agenda, but she couldn't understand what that could be.

Jalaluddin stood near the entrance of Anjali's container for some time. He then started talking about his role as an advisor and the time when he started his consultancy. Anjali was getting uncomfortable. Her colleagues were slated to return to their homes very soon. The last class had just finished, and most of them picked up their dinner from the canteen on their way back to their containers. What if they saw Jalaluddin standing here in the international housing where he didn't belong instead of going back to his home? She was getting restless thinking about the stories people might cook up seeing him here. She decided to invite him in instead of standing outside.

'Would you like to step in and have a cup of tea, perhaps? I am not so much of a coffee person.'

'I thought you would never invite me, and I am not a coffee person either. A cup of Indian chai would be very good.'

'I don't make typical Indian chai. I have it black and maybe without sugar. I don't think it will be according to your taste or liking.'

'Do you care about my taste or liking?' Jalaluddin moved close to Anjali as they both tried to go in through the narrow door at the same time. He realized that her face flushed, and he stepped aside although their bodies brushed against each other. Anjali entered the room, kept her keys in the basket and pretended to get busy. She pulled the tea maker, noisily opened the tin where she kept her assorted tea bags and turned towards the tap to fill up the kettle.

'You can sit down and make the tea a little later. I am not in a hurry to go home … unless you want to throw me out,' he laughed. 'There are a whole lot of kids at home, my nieces and nephews. Getting some me-time is rare in that house. It's very chaotic, although I love each one of those brats as mine.'

He started moving around, picking up things that were kept on the table, which served as a writing desk and her dinner table.

'You never had kids? You would have been such a loving mother.'

'How do you know that? We barely know each other.'

'When I look at someone, I know. I have this special power, like a yogi (he laughed again). I know you are very kind and loving. I knew it the first time I saw you alighting from the SUV, the day you joined and came to Kabul.

'Was that your husband? He was a handsome man; may peace be upon him. I heard about his demise; I am so sorry. You were very pretty then. This must be your wedding photo? You are gorgeous even now, very pretty.

'You know my favourite Hindi song, "*Chaudahnvi ka Chand ho* … something, something …" I thought that song should have been written for you, absolutely, word for word.'

He started humming '*Hothon pe khelti hui tabassum ki bijliyan* …' in a low tune.

Anjali desperately wanted to normalize the situation; she placed the tray with the teacups on the table a bit noisily. Jalal sat down on the sofa and smiled at her.

'My Hindi is bad, and my voice is equally bad. I hope you didn't mind my humming something off-tune. Why don't you sit down? I just hope I am not making you uncomfortable. Let's sit and talk. You know, when I heard about your husband, I thought about my mother. It was the same kidney failure, those traumatic days of dialysis, her sinking and my helplessness.'

His voice choked, and Anjali thought his eyes had become moist, but she was unsure how to react. Jalal came forward, placed his hand on her hand and whispered, 'I understand you; I do. I share your grief; we have come together in grief. I want to remain here, beside you, as your best friend. Would you accept me as your friend?'

Anjali gulped, emotions forming a tight knot in her throat. She picked up the cup and took a sip, desperately trying to calm the storm that was swelling in her bosom. Her lips quivered as she said, 'Tell me more about your mother, your life, your childhood.'

'You want to hear it all today? Maybe some today, some another day when I drive you through the city and we go for a long ride? I have a soft-skinned, black-coloured SUV and I love to drive. I can show you something about our beloved Kabul.'

'Are we allowed to go out? I went with Dr Cathy the other day. We had to return within three hours.'

Jalal waved his slender fingers in the air, 'Don't worry, if I ask for permission, they will allow you to go with me. Nothing special about the tension; it is always there. We grew up seeing it hanging from the trees and lamp posts, lurking in the corner.'

They spoke for some more time and chatted about their home, their past and their loved ones.

Jalal got up, 'I must go now. I wish I didn't have to go. This is a beautiful evening; it will be etched in my mind forever as the start of a friendship. The tea was lovely, and so were you. Can

I tell you something, and you will hear this often from me: you are precious, very precious to me.'

Saying this, he left, just like that. No handshakes, no salaam, he just walked out of the room. Anjali was baffled and stuck to the floor where she stood. She stood there for a long time, the door swaying in the breeze with a creaking noise.

Long after he left, something stayed with Anjali. The way he behaved, trying to be caring and tender … Anjali was reminded of a feeling she had forgotten.

Once he disappeared from her sight, she broke down. Sitting at her dining table, she cried for a long time. She missed Abhay so much and hated Jalaluddin for stirring those emotions in her once more.

Had her husband been with her, men like this wouldn't have tried to take advantage of her situation. She had always felt protected and loved by her husband. Despite his ill health and all the challenges that they had faced in life, his protective arm was always around her. His tight grip held her hand all the time.

She slowly got up and went back to change. Yesterday, she had contacted the Indian embassy. They confirmed that they were getting ready for evacuation. They asked her to come over but regretted that they could not arrange a pickup as cars were being used to pick up other Indians stuck in different provinces for evacuation. She would ask the security director for a drop, but she couldn't decide when. Should she leave the campus and go tomorrow? Like others, she too wanted to be here till it was confirmed that evacuation was the only option.

She started packing her suitcase and a duffle bag. As she packed, she gently put in Abhay's picture, wrapping it up with his T-shirt that she always carried.

The evening was free, suddenly there was not much to do with no classes and uncertainty looming large. The evening was as empty as her mind was, which went completely blank sitting on the sofa with a book. She didn't even pick it up to read, but it was lying on her lap while tears kept streaking down her cheeks.

It seemed every house had someone packing something, wrapping precious things with pieces of cloth or paper, and keeping them safe. A whole city on the verge of departure, planning and preparing for an escape.

◈

There was no scope for relaxation in Zohra's life. She was either working at the university or working at home. Yet, on Friday, she and her husband stole some time off and went to see a Bollywood movie, roamed in the park basking in the fading colours of dusk and went for an ice cream. This Friday was different for her, maybe different for everyone in Kabul. They were going about the usual routine, but their thoughts were occupied with apprehensions of what was next. Work was divided at the breakfast table. Zohra went to the market with her mother and sister-in-law to pick up dry fruits, biscuits, spices and other household items that they needed to stock. 'I need as many hands as possible' was her mother-in-law's diktat.

The scanty news that was trickling in was painting a very grim picture of the country. Kunduz and Sar-e Pol had been captured by the Taliban after a heavy clash with the Afghan National Army soldiers. The battle for Kunduz had started as early as June, and now the Taliban elite shock troops had captured all the important locations involving the freeing of the prisoners, who were ex-soldiers from the earlier Taliban regime. Things did not look good, and people were speculating which province would succumb to their might next.

It was decided that Zohra's husband would go to pick up money from the ATMs. He had planned to visit several of them till he reached the withdrawal limit. He would also take his father's ATM card. They needed enough cash to last them a couple of months. His father and his brother would go to the wholesaler to pick up sacks of rice, flour and sugar. Zohra was given several shopping bags to carry and lots of instructions.

The market was tense. People were buying groceries in bulk, negotiating furiously, and loading their vehicles. The heat and the apprehension of trouble made everyone irritable; fights broke out and people were shouting and jostling. Zohra and her family were back home, exhausted. As she sat near the window with a cup of green tea, she decided that it was now or never. She would take advantage of the chaos and leave with her husband.

Zohra had a bag packed in which she had kept both her and her husband's clothes, their passport, money and some valuable trinkets. As she was packing, her husband looked at her helplessly; his eyes showed that he wanted to ask a lot of questions. Perhaps he feared leaving the familiar. Zohra didn't want to give him a chance to reconsider. She just put the bag aside, sighed and said, 'Let's go to sleep. Who knows what the next day has in store for us?'

Nadia felt safe in the knowledge that her packed bag was already on the campus. Today, she looked at the house with a special curiosity, as if trying to soak in the picture of the place that could have been her dream house but turned into her prison. She traced her finger on the walls and the design of the carpet and smiled to herself that she was not going to miss any of them.

◈

Fawzia tried to explain the ongoing situation in the country to her son, which he hardly understood, but blinked his small eyes while chewing on the biscuit that his mother had brought on her way home. Fawzia had no one to consult, every decision would be her decision. To survive, to earn a living and to feed her son, she would have to work, and that she could do once she left her country. She decided to get help from the university and go somewhere else where she could survive with dignity. She, too, kept a bag packed, pushed under the bed.

Those who were planning to leave made phone calls to their near and dear ones, with tear-soaked emotional speeches. Neighbours opened their doors and hugged each other. Jars and boxes were emptied, several delicacies were cooked to empty the kitchen, and the food was shared amongst all. Televisions and sofas wore a white shroud or the shroud of some old, printed bed sheets with faded flower motifs.

Over a million people were preparing to escape, in search of a haven, away from all that was once precious to them. Their love and their dreams were built together with their partners and families. All was to be left behind while they were gone for a long time, with no certain date of return.

Part III

FARAR: THE ESCAPE

2

With hardly any students or staff members, the campus was quiet. There were no local workers, no gardeners, just two people manning the canteen and a few retired guards from the Indian army who worked with the security agency. They were strolling around with their huge guns on their shoulders, ready for any combat.

People were mostly confined to their apartments or containers, quietly sipping a cup of tea or making a toast or two to eat. It seemed that everyone had lost their appetite overnight. Hardly anyone was seen around the canteen. Some were busy clearing their desks and cupboards, while others were folding and wrapping their favourite wall hanging or pushing the photo frame of their loved ones into their tiny suitcase or backpack. Everyone was still hoping that things would become normal later and they'd all be back to their idyllic campus life.

And then suddenly, in the afternoon, all the phones started buzzing, with one text:

'Kind attention of all faculty and staff members. Please destroy everything that could associate you with this university. Delete files that have the university's logo, change your password and delete messages from your chat boxes. Limit your social media presence and save your name as someone else's.'

What followed was utter confusion. Did they mean that one needed to log off from all e-learning platforms? Delete assignments that have the logo pasted on each page and slide? Move out of social media and block or delete the students because they could be identified? How would they remain connected? What had happened for all this to be done? Endless questions, endless comments and endless suggestions were on every faculty and staff member's mind.

Anjali walked over to Dr Cathy's room and decided to seek her help in both tasks—in deleting information, as asked, and to discuss Professor Jalaluddin, who had been messaging her incessantly.

Cathy was kind and patient with her. She showed her which files to delete and which to keep. As she offered a nice cup of tea to a much-harrowed Anjali, she decided to talk about Jalaluddin.

'He is an intelligent man, but he has a weakness for women. In the past, too, he has befriended many women on the campus and tried to develop intimacy with them. He has been known to send many messages, sometimes even thirty to forty messages a day. It is best to avoid him politely. Now is not the time to deal with such issues, or we could have reported this to the ethics committee on grounds of harassment.

'You will find plenty of men like him here—harmless, lonely souls who find momentary excitement in talking to a so-called "emancipated woman". We are independent, earn our living, don't cover our heads or toes, and we are confident and bold—not qualities they associate with women. Naturally, we evoke a sense of wonder. Unless he is making lewd remarks or trying to harm you, you have nothing to worry about.

'I guess you have led a shielded life with your husband and have not dealt with such hungry wolves, as I have. I know them well. Soon, we will be out of this place, and who knows whether we will ever return? So, don't worry so much.

'I have seen it all. Married twice and thrown out by those same men I loved and who inflicted severe wounds on my body and soul. So, believe me when I say, this too shall pass.'

Anjali thanked her for the encouragement and went back to her room. On the way, she suddenly stopped on the tracks as she saw a huge fire with thick black smoke billowing near the community centre. Students who were still staying at the dormitory were running helter-skelter. They were carrying files, books and hard disks and throwing them into the fire. A few were pushing what was thrown towards the engulfing flame with small iron rods. They were following the instructions of the chief information officer to burn all that they could containing any names, addresses or email IDs connected to the university.

Fights had intensified around Mazar-i-Sharif between the Taliban and the government forces. The Taliban forces had occupied the police headquarters and the prison. Part of Badakhshan province had fallen into their hands, and news agencies had confirmed the capture of the Kunduz airport. No one knew what would happen next.

Noor, a young undergraduate, stopped in front of Anjali and asked, 'Ma'am, do you have anything to burn? I can collect it from your room. Things are very bad. I don't know what is going to happen to us, I am scared.'

Anjali couldn't find the right words to assure this young lad. She mustered up the courage to encourage him, 'Don't worry, we are there. Education will not stop; things will be okay. You will graduate this year and be careful of the fire. Don't go too near.'

Was Noor convinced? His small pale face didn't show that, yet he managed to muster up a half-hearted smile and said, 'It's okay. Ma'am, our country has seen worse. This, too, shall pass. You be all right, ma'am. Let me know if you need anything. These things are new to you. I can understand what you must be feeling.' He smiled once more and ran towards the office building to gather more files and papers.

Anjali stood near the canteen for a while, thinking that while her life was riddled with pain and grief, it was better than this young man's, whose future seemed so unsure. He was barely in his twenties and had already seen so much. This is what made him calm and composed in the face of adversity. Such situations try us all, and only the brave survive.

Taking small, slow steps, she decided to go to the canteen. Hunger and the desire to eat had long left her but she did not want to be alone. Slowly, others started drifting in. There were a lot of animated discussions taking place at the tables. Fawzia was standing quietly nearby, absorbing all that was being discussed eagerly. Zohra, who usually didn't come to the canteen, accompanied the registrar today. She was asking the maximum number of questions.

'How will we go out? What kind of arrangements are there? Will we head directly to the airport? Will we all stay in the safe house inside the campus waiting for it to tide over?'

No one had any concrete answer, everything was mere speculation. Bits and pieces of information were floating about everywhere.

'We will all be taken to the US embassy.'

'A helicopter, probably a Chinook, will land at our field, and we will all board that.'

'No helicopter can land. The airport will be the first thing that the Taliban will control. Are you talking about the Bagram airbase? Isn't it empty?'

'We need to contact our embassy and ask them to help us.'

'Embassies have evacuated their staff. Who will help us?'

'We have enough rations to stay on campus for a month.'

'It is not safe; they will blow us out with bazookas and rockets!'

The smell of burnt plastic and paper hung heavily in the atmosphere. Their eyes were burning from the billowing black smoke, and the whole ambience was eerie and uncomfortable. *How much paper does a university have?* All gathered over the years, the burning and throwing into the fire didn't stop for long, and it was already dusk.

A few hours later, there was a loud knock echoing through the corridors. Parvez, who worked as an errand boy in the faculty accommodation, was banging on all the doors frantically.

A few seconds passed and everyone peeped out with anxiety written all over their faces.

'What happened, Parvez? Why are you knocking on the doors at this hour? Have we been attacked?'

'Madam, Sir, I don't have time to explain. Please grab your emergency bag and come towards the gate. We need to escape now, at this very moment. Please don't delay, we must leave at once.'

'Wait, wait, who told you this?'

'Where are we going to go at this hour?!'

'No flight is scheduled now! I don't think the airport will be operational at this time. Where are we supposed to go?'

'We cannot leave like this! We need some time! Who is guiding this operation?'

Parvez was faced with a barrage of questions and angry faces. Some were visibly angry and screaming their heads off. Some stood still while others shook their head gravely. The poor boy didn't have any answers. He was just doing what he had been asked to do.

Exasperated, he just said, 'The cars will leave in exactly thirty minutes. Everyone is to gather their belongings and wait in front of the iron gate. You can ask the university leaders. They are all leaving with you. I need to go and pack my bag, too. I hope to be with you on this journey, and I hope we will stay safe.' Saying this, he hurried towards the dormitory where he stayed.

People stood there for some more time, debating and in shock. The air was heavy with apprehension and a sense of foreboding.

Suddenly, it hit Anjali, and she started feeling unwell. A sudden sensation of tightening in her chest was followed by her limbs feeling paralysed. Her tongue felt heavy and her mouth was filled with a metallic taste. She had faced this situation before, in front of the ICU, when Abhay's life was ebbing away.

This was deja vu.

She stood there for a while till someone shouted at her, 'Anjali, go, go, get your bag, fast! We are about to leave.' She suddenly woke up from her stupor and rushed inside. She grabbed her bag and pushed a packet of biscuits, a few apples and a water bottle inside. There wasn't much space for anything else.

She threw one last look at her container, her haven for the last few months. As she closed the door, pushing the keys into her denim pocket, inane questions crowded her mind: Does this key need to be handed over? Is there a register to sign like when the keys were given to me? She didn't know; she quickened her pace towards the iron gate and saw her colleagues a few steps ahead or behind her. There were thirteen of them.

Three Land Cruisers were lined up, the same bulletproof vehicles that were sent for them when they had first arrived. Dr Watson nodded at them, and the security supervisors, Samim and Ahmad, were urging people to squeeze into the cars.

Suddenly, a commotion erupted nearby. Nadia, Fawzia and Zohra, with her husband, were standing there with their bags. They were insisting on being taken with the expatriate members.

A heated discussion was taking place in the local language with the head of operations, who was refusing their request flatly. Nadia was sobbing, and Fawzia was tugging her son towards the car.

Someone from a car made a rude comment, 'Ah, what do they want now, to be taken with us abroad? Their greed seems to be endless. Go look after your own country and be with your countrymen and let us go. We are not a part of you and never were. Just get the hell out of here and do not delay us. You will not protect us when your brothers come to butcher us, just GO!'

Cathy and Anjali turned to see what was happening, but suddenly the driver sat in the car and started the engine, and a gush of black smoke covered the glass. They couldn't see much, and the sound of the engine silenced the conversation. As crosses were drawn and hands raised in prayer, everyone surrendered their fate to the hands of this driver.

Part IV

FARAR KON: RUN AWAY

3

The road from the university was long and winding like a maze. All three of the convoy cars had navigated the first part of the lane when they came to a halt, faced with rows of security personnel lining up to block their path. These guards were from a private organization. Some of them were familiar faces who used to smile at the faculty and staff when they met each other on campus. However, there were no smiling faces today. Their stern expressions showed that they meant business.

On seeing the cars, two of their senior members approached the first car to talk to the leadership team. The security guards looked angry. There was an animated conversation between the president, the operations officer and the two guards. They were shaking their heads violently and the president was trying to placate them by placing his hand on their shoulders.

Mark, one of the English teachers who was in the car with Anjali, Cathy and Nadia stepped out to find out what was going on and what the delay was all about.

After a couple of minutes, he came back with a grave expression.

'They won't allow us to go unless their dues are paid. They worry that they might not get their salary as the university will now be abandoned. Our president received news from trusted sources that Kandahar, Herat and Lashkargah would probably fall into the hands of the Taliban by tomorrow, if not today. With Herat succumbing, the fight is nearly over. People were expecting that the Resistance force would put up a big fight in Panjshir. They, too, have lost. There is no hope. It is just a matter of time before they march in through the Kabul gates. There is a rumour that the political head may just hand over the power to them.

'The guards are scared like us. They want to flee. They all want to go home, and they want their salary. I am not too sure how salaries can be paid at this moment. Let's see what happens. It seems to be a bad start.'

Cathy, who wasn't in a great mood, asked, 'Who told them? Someone must have informed them of our leaving the campus. It must have taken them some time to regroup at the exit. If we face hostility from those who are supposed to protect us, then I don't know what to expect in the next few hours or days that lie ahead.'

Parvez came towards their car in a couple of minutes and spoke in a hushed tone.

'It's all settled; they are allowing us to go. They were permitted to take what they wished from the campus. The president has signed a declaration that in the next fifteen days their salary would be arranged and transferred to them. We can go now. I have been asked to convey it to the members in all the cars, so please do not worry.'

Anjali looked shocked. 'Did he just say that the guards are permitted to take what they wish from the campus? Does it mean that they will have access to our rooms and take our belongings, too? I have a lot of things that were handpicked by my late husband. They are precious to me. Could we not have shipped them when there was still time? As far as I remember, the threat of the Taliban taking over has been looming large since May, since the withdrawal of the American and NATO troops. It doesn't make any sense.'

Cathy replied irritably, 'Well, nothing makes sense. We all signed up for teaching, and we did it voluntarily. We should have known that this is a volatile region. Anything can happen here any day. Some six months back, ten rockets were fired at the airport. One of the local airlines' planes was destroyed. This is a dangerous place to work, and we were all aware of it. No one was expecting that the provinces would fall so quickly; everyone thought that it would be a long-drawn battle and perhaps contained once again by foreign forces. Maybe it is a good idea not to have precious belongings in a place like this.'

Mark added, 'I heard that the campus would be handed over to the Taliban as per the negotiations. If that is the case, this is the last time we will see this place. None of us are coming back.'

'Who told you? From where have you heard this?' asked Anjali.

'That young guy who has just come to teach. That thin, lanky one in spectacles, he is supposed to be well connected politically, has some kind of alliance.'

The cars started moving slowly and everyone kept silent, perhaps saving their energy and bracing themselves for the journey ahead. Everyone realized that reaching home was not going to be very easy.

Finally, the cars were on the road, moving as noiselessly as possible, in a convoy, coiling like a snake and slithering in lanes and by-lanes, trying to avoid the main road which by now was dark due to power cuts, and an eerie silence prevailed all around.

No one knew the destination—the question of where they were going was looming large, but no one had any answer or any idea about who to ask.

◈

The trees looked forlorn and sad. A few vendors were selling nuts and fruits standing at the roadside with a worried look, frowning and impatient to sell their wares and go back to the safety of their homes, if any home was still safe. The cars passed the bus depot. Even from inside the safety of the car, the sense of urgency was palpable in the people getting on the bus. People were rushing into buses with whatever belongings they could grab while the buses waited with their engines on.

News of Ghazni falling had sent shock waves across the world. The city lies on the Kabul-Kandahar highway and serves as a gateway between Kabul and the southern provinces. With Ghazni being captured, the road to Kabul was clear for the Taliban. A proposal for power-sharing by the central government had been rejected by the Taliban. They were looking for full control. The Shindand air base in Herat was also captured, along with two Black Hawks, the four-bladed military utility helicopters stationed there. Everything was happening in an accelerated way now. What people thought would take months, if not years, was happening within hours. There was only one thought on everyone's mind: to move away from all this and look for a safe place.

The driver explained that people had started escaping; everyone was going back to their provinces—Wardak, Panjshir or Bamiyan and beyond. The journey would be perilous.

The meandering road seemed never-ending, and the journey was tedious and laden with apprehension. Apart from some heavy vehicles and large cars filled with people zooming past, the road was clear, maybe a bit too clear for an evening when it should usually be filled with those returning home from work. After an hour or so, suddenly, the cars lined up in front of a gate.

The iron gates opened with a screech. Inside, there were several buildings, each barely three-storeys high. There was a vast field in the centre and small hut-like buildings all around it in the farthest corner. From what could be seen with the help of floodlights, it looked like a training camp or a military base.

As everyone alighted from the cars, there seemed to be other people who had also just arrived. All of them were expatriates except a few locals who had come with the crowd from the university. Everyone needed to stretch their legs after sitting for more than an hour in a cramped car. They huddled in one place, looking around, trying to find where exactly they were and what this place was.

Very soon, their curiosity was put to rest when the president of the university gathered them around and announced:

'This is a safe place; this compound belongs to the Daring Eagles. They are security providers to most foreign agencies and embassies in Kabul, including ours. They will be hosting most of the expats for the time being, till we can find our way to the airport and avail of the special military planes. The arrangement is nothing great, but basic.

'The facility is not meant for hosting guests; these are for the ex-soldiers who are working for the agency. I am sorry we are unable to provide anything better than this. We know we will all be safe here; at least that is our hope. Please keep your phones charged and in network mode so that you don't miss any communication.

'I also urge you not to venture out and to confine yourself to the rooms allotted to you. For the first two days, we will all have to be in the basement. Once things settle down, we will be given proper rooms on a shared basis. Try to be with your group so that we have a head count every day.'

Before the president could complete his briefing, a commando-looking person came and asked the men and women to be segregated.

Zohra, who had been holding her husband's hand tightly all this while, visibly uncomfortable amidst a bunch of unfamiliar people, was now alarmed by this directive. She refused to let go of her husband's hand. 'He came here because of me! He knows no one except me. I cannot be separated from him. Please! He needs to stay with me. No, no, he needs to be with me!'

The commando-looking guy was unfazed by her hysterical pleading. He came forward and said, 'I am sorry, ma'am, this is not allowed. There are several other families. They are being separated, too. Only infants are allowed to stay with their mothers, not their husbands.

'You can meet each other in two days. Once we know what is happening.'

Zohra tried to persuade and plead, but seeing that the officer wasn't going to budge, she let go of her husband's hand after explaining things to him in Pashto. Her husband looked very uneasy, but understood that there was no other way.

No one bothered comforting him; everyone was busy trying to fathom their own next move for survival.

Fawzia, too, was told to let her son be with the other group of men. He seemed to be a friendly boy and was soon chatting away with a man from the group. Parvez promised Fawzia to look after him.

Once everyone was divided into two groups, men on one side and women on the other, they all lined up and started moving to the building, which looked slightly bigger than the rest. Everyone was clutching their bags tightly, standing in a long line like obedient students following orders without question.

4

The women were led by a younger commando, who was in full gear with his AK-47, magazines and hand grenades. He resembled someone who had come straight from the battlefield. He was a man of very few words and believed in expressing himself through gestures. He kept pointing them towards a corridor, and then the next, the one after that, and when the corridors ended, he pointed towards a staircase that looked like it was leading down towards the basement. It did feel like he was leading them into a deep, dark abyss, a pitiless bottom of no return, but they followed him silently.

As they descended the winding staircase, their journey came to a grinding halt in front of a large iron door. The door was unlocked, and the musty smell of coffee and cigarettes hit everyone, almost throwing them into nausea. The windows were tightly shut and sealed. The smell floated out of the room after a while, once the slow-whirling fans were switched on.

The place was chilly despite the hot August weather outside the room. Someone commented that it was cold, to which the commander answered that the refrigeration system for the supplies was in the basement; perhaps that is why it felt cold and wet.

The room was not well lit, with only a few low-voltage tube lights, which were making the shadows take on a ghostly appearance. There was the same eerie silence all around; all that could be heard was the cautious footsteps of the group as they shuffled and dragged their feet, getting their bearings in this large room. They were all tired by now, and the uncertainty made them wearier.

Had they been on campus, the lights would have been switched off and people would have been cozily tucked into their beds with air conditioners whizzing away, secure in the peace that engulfed them.

But this wasn't the cozy campus. This place was slightly better than a prison cell. It was barren with no furniture, just white-washed walls and a dusty cement floor.

The commander pointed to a stack of old newspapers kept on the floor, 'These are your sheets or mattresses for tonight. There was no time to get anything better, tomorrow we shall try and get a few mattresses from our dormitory. I am sorry it is going to be uncomfortable, but we have no alternative.

'We are trying to maintain the impression that no one is here. So please try and be as quiet as possible, and if you must talk, do so in whispers. I will try and bring some food. We don't have cooked food, so you will get some fruit and biscuits for the night.'

There were around forty to fifty women in this room. Some sighed, some complained and some were just confused about the situation.

'If they had planned for us to stay here, they should have made some arrangements.'

'How can we spend the whole night on a bare floor which feels wet and cold? We are not young; we have weak bones.'

'I think my lungs might get affected, maybe some kind of infection or pneumonia. I am sure there would be no medical help at all. This is so lame!'

'What is this room? Some kind of holding place? Is it meant for prisoners?'

'Must be a storeroom. I guess we are no better than beggars, or worse!'

After some time, everyone receded into silence. There was no one to listen to them: the commander had left as noiselessly as he had come.

All the women slowly moved around, trying to acquaint themselves with this place. They broke into small groups with their friends and acquaintances, and some settled down on the floor, putting extra sheets of newspaper to rest their tired bodies.

Cathy, Anjali, Zohra, Fawzia and Nadia came together. Both Zohra and Fawzia were worried about being separated from their family.

'He has never stayed alone; I am always there with him.' Fawzia was worried about her son.

Zohra, regretting her decision of bringing her husband with her, said, 'I dragged my husband into all this by promising him a better future in Canada. It's all my fault, or else we would have been sleeping in his warm and soft bed by now. I hope I am going to be able to give him what I have promised. The dreams that I showed him every night—the Canadian dream.'

Cathy and Anjali had different thoughts in their minds. They had not left anyone behind, nor was anyone waiting for them or worrying about their safety. They just rested their heads on the wall, tilted their necks and tried to listen to all that was being said by people around them.

While others spoke in hushed tones, Nadia suddenly started sobbing. She hid her face on her knees and sobbed for a long time. No coaxing or request would make her say what was bothering her. Her body trembled with sobs.

After a while, she looked up, still shivering as she tried to wipe away her tears with the back of her palm. 'I am so scared, so very scared.

'I am running away from home; I have not told anyone. They must be looking for me. I just told my friend Breshna about my plan. I am scared for her. I hope they don't torture her to tell the truth, and if she does, I am dead. I have brought dishonour to my husband and his family, and to my family too. I will never be accepted by any of them. If they find me, they will perhaps stone me to death or whip me and throw me in prison on account of sin. I have committed zena. I know my husband would be the first one to take up the whip or throw the first stone at me. Oh! What did I do? Why couldn't I be like other women, enduring everything silently?'

She was cold with fear, and her face looked ashen. She shuddered as she spoke about her husband, about the endless torture she had endured in his hands. She added that she had switched off her phone and was relying on her professors and colleagues to guide her through.

Anjali patted her head and asked, 'Where will you go all alone? Do you have any plans? Have you thought about the journey from here? We are all going back home, but I am not sure about you and Fawzia. What are your plans?'

'Madam, I have been corresponding with rescue agencies secretly. They will take us to Doha, and we will be kept in a refugee camp till we manage to procure our visa for the US. I don't know about Fawzia, but I have contacted Dr Kaufmann. Do you remember her, Dr Cathy?' she turned to look at Cathy. 'She was the chair of the department and retired a while back. She is very fond of me and treats me like her own daughter. I have been keeping her posted.

'Dr Kaufmann said she would help me once I reached the US and perhaps arrange a scholarship so that I can resume my studies. I am carrying all my certificates with me. I will not be able to breathe easily until I am out of the country. I am going to leave my past behind and start afresh. I want to become something, will I, Dr Cathy?'

She kept looking at Cathy. 'Will I make it big in the world outside, where women are not beaten up every day for being a woman?'

As her last sentence hung in the silence that engulfed them, Cathy knew she needed to say something to this frightened girl; any words of encouragement would do at such a time.

'Yes, my dear, you will, you are a very brave girl. If you have come this far, you surely will realize your dreams. You have the courage, and you are intelligent, what more does one need?'

Fawzia whispered in her broken English, 'The NGO which gave me a new leg is in Ireland, I will go there. They promised to get me an education and a job and get my Arzoo, a school. I want a good school. Arzoo is very bright. I miss my father and mother. Father helps me. Help my son. Helped me when my leg was gone, my husband gone, he helped. I earn money, then I will take them.'

What started with a frightened girl's plea for a new and free life now became a time for everyone to affirm their path ahead. Cathy spoke a little about herself and her family, and Anjali did the same. They both wanted to continue teaching online till the university opened again, perhaps in another country. Unlike Fawzia and Nadia, for both of them, their work was what life was about—no children, no parents, no husband, no family whatsoever.

◈

Time passed slowly, and each hour seemed endless. After a while, the commander came back with some other people, carrying plastic bags with biscuits, apples, bananas, dry cake and water bottles. They were generous in distributing them.

Nadia and Fawzia took two extra packets and kept them in their bags, and added that they were saving this for tomorrow, as nobody knew if they would get their next meal.

Everyone ate very quietly, and there was not much choice. The commander showed them their way to the toilet, urging them to keep it clean as everyone would be using the same.

It was already past midnight; around six hours had passed sitting on the cold floor. The tired bodies settled in for some rest, some of them slumped, others curled up on the floor, while some sat with their backs to the wall and legs spread in front. Some used their bags as makeshift pillows.

Anjali looked at her phone's screensaver. Abhay was still smiling at her, and she sighed and told him to reduce the waiting period in this dungeon for her. Stillness descended in the room, and all that could be heard was a light snoring, the shifting of legs and the rustling of clothes and the newspaper on the floor. The night faded into the morning, and the ghostly shadows became less ghastly. The wait seemed endless, as if these forgotten souls were condemned to be here forever.

Sunlight couldn't enter the room, so the time was anybody's guess. Slowly, everyone woke up and tried to stand up and stretch themselves, shaking off the creaking of bones and groans.

It must have been seven in the morning when piles of toast, hard-boiled eggs, bananas, tea in thermos flasks and paper cups, and plates were brought down by two helpers from the camp.

The commander announced that Mazar-I-Sharif, Ghor province and a few other places were now captured by the Taliban. There was news that they had also entered Maidan-e-Wardak, and rumour had it that they had encircled Kabul. The good news was that the US and UK governments had deployed troops to airlift their officials. The news was confirmed that chartered flights would take the nationals of their country out of Kabul. The question that remained was how and when? The evacuation would prioritize diplomatic staff; would they even count those working for various aid agencies or educational institutions? Besides, everyone had the same thought: when would the Taliban enter the gate of Kabul city, the Dar-Waze-Shahr?

The group was informed that they still needed to be in the room and only towards the evening, after observing the chain of events, would they be allocated rooms on a shared basis.

'We don't know whether the Taliban will be hostile and if they will attack our campus. If they do, then they will butcher all of us, and they won't spare the women. This is not accommodation befitting the ladies, and we understand that. We are holding the men in a similar arrangement in another room.

'I know you all are going through a living hell, sitting the whole night on a bare floor with no proper food and a toilet. We sincerely apologize. We are taking these measures only to protect you. We need to hide you as we don't want informers selling us out to the Taliban, and we hope we are successful in our endeavour, and God is going to be with us. Let us all pray for that. I shall come down and brief you intermittently.'

The group was not in a frame of mind to ask them questions. No one was in the mood to indulge in small talk. Trying to sleep was the only option that was being tried by many, which might help them wait for the evening to come. If they were lucky, they might get a bed to sleep in at night.

The phone charging point was the most precious thing in that whole room. Although the internet connection was weak, it was the only saving grace apart from the earphones that each one was carrying.

Fawzia and Zohra were restless as they requested several times to see their son and husband, and each time their request was turned down. Anjali kept looking at the photos saved on her phone, reminding her of her lost happy days, while Cathy was keen to follow the BBC. They were hardly talking to each other, and when their eyes met, it was a polite nod or a smile, that's all.

5

It had been more than eighteen hours since everyone had been sitting on the floor, eating what was being handed to them, and waiting for news that would decide their fate.

There was nothing to do after breakfast; no new discussions, no new stories—all had been said and heard. The only thing that could be heard was the restless shifting of papers, the rustling of bags or clothes and the intermittent sighing of people. Some people would accidentally increase the volume of the online news or a song being played on their phone, and everyone would turn around to hear it eagerly. Some tried to follow the news very diligently, or shouted across the hall if they heard about any new development.

Anjali spoke after a while, 'I think we made a big mistake by delaying our departure. The university is such an island; no news comes from outside unless someone volunteers to bring it in. We should have gone much earlier or not returned when the semester started. We never had such issues earlier. There should have been a drill.'

Cathy was still very irritable. No one was doing well mentally, but she showed visible signs of being angry. She spat out. 'And your Jalal, what happened to him? Disappeared! Never helped, it seemed. He could have at least provided us with the correct information! For you, at least, if not for us. He could have protected his "madam". He seems to be full of s**t.'

Anjali was shocked at her rudeness. She kept quiet for a few seconds, gulped down the insult and just said, 'I don't know why you are picking on him. Why are you even involving me with him? I am polite with him as I am with you all. Anyway, now is not the time to discuss such things. We have other pressing things at hand. We just need to keep our sanity.'

Cathy grunted and decided to look at the wall on the opposite side of the room.

It was around 11 a.m. when another commander came to take all of them outside. The sudden rays of sunlight blinded them. The first thing they did was to fill their lungs with fresh air; it was such a relief to be out of that cold and dark dungeon.

'The Taliban has taken over Kabul; you can hear the gunshots. We have learnt that the Pul-e-Charkhi prison has been thrown open and there is mayhem on the streets. There is no power supply. People are killing and trampling each other to reach the airport. Everything is mixed up; no one can tell a citizen from a convict. There are rumours that the president has surrendered his power and left the country.

'The news of all of you hiding here has reached the ears of the Taliban leaders. I don't know how they came to know, but someone from here must have told one of their informants. It doesn't matter who told whom; what matters is the consequence.

Hence, confining you all to the basement is not going to help. We cannot pretend that you don't exist anymore; you do, and they are aware of it.

'We will try our best to defend the camp and every member hiding in it. Rooms will be allocated to you, two or three people per room, and you can wash before lunch, which is served in the canteen. We have volunteers to help you with your room and show you the way to the canteen. Please feel free to walk around in the field and make up for the lost exercise of these two days.' Some more instructions followed, and some more queries were answered, but nothing about the way forward was discussed in much detail.

As the whole group gathered, Fawzia and Zohra rushed to see their family. Anjali, Cathy and Nadia moved to a room that was meant for them to share. It was a bare room with three cots, each with a pillow and a blanket. A table had a jug of water, and there was a chair to sit on, and that was it, no other furniture.

The three bundled their bags at the head of the bed and went to lie down. A bed with a pillow felt like heaven. Very soon, they dozed off to sleep, peacefully and in a deep slumber. Mental exhaustion had tired them out.

They would have continued sleeping had it not been for Fawzia and Zohra, who came to call them for lunch, banging on their door. Groggily, they got up and went to the dining hall. It seemed that the commanders were trying to make up for the last night and this morning.

The spread was huge, with Kabuli pulao, dumplings, spaghetti, fried chicken wings, bread pudding, fruits and juices—the entire length of the table was covered with food.

They met their colleagues who were housed in the men's section, and after a cursory exchange of greetings, they all got down to eat.

Some were cruel and joked about it as the 'Last Supper', others said, 'Thank god I won't be beheaded on an empty stomach'—light humour lined with the darkness of impending trouble. Everyone made use of the spread, and soon the table was nearly empty.

After lunch, they were allowed to roam around and bask in the warm sun. The sun, which was unbearable a few days back, now appeared to be so friendly and welcoming after a night in a damp and cold cellar. People huddled in groups, chatting among themselves. Seeing them, one couldn't guess that these people were fleeing for their lives. They looked like friends catching up with each other.

The atmosphere was light and friendly, and the university folks went around befriending those from NGOs and embassies.

'This is the power of a full belly,' Anjali said as she looked around.

The commander who met them when they arrived remarked, 'Madam, we do have the provision for feeding you all for a month; after that, don't draw your dagger at us.' Everyone laughed as though giddy from the sun and fresh air.

The evening was spent in aimlessness, roaming around in the field. They watched the walking and training of the forty-odd army dogs walking in a line. Coffee and tea were readily available, so everyone was enjoying that.

During dinner in the canteen, it was announced that everyone should be present at the main ground at 3 a.m.

People were asked to come with their belongings as a few Chinook helicopters were expected to come and airlift some people to the airport.

As soon as this was announced, pandemonium broke loose.

'Who will be going, who is on the list, and who is not?'

'Are these planes departing from the airport? Which country are they going to?'

'If they take us to some other country, how will we go back home? We don't have the visa or much cash in hand to get tickets or hotels. We would be entering illegally.'

'Who is going to inform us? Is this plan backed by some government agency?'

The two commanders tried to answer as well as they could, but soon left exasperated, knowing this confusion would not abate, whatever they said. The group discussed and debated among themselves as they slowly started moving towards their rooms. All the while, gunshots and more could be heard outside the boundary wall; they were not too far off now.

As the night progressed, the sound of gunshots and missiles being fired grew louder in the quietness of the night, and everyone had a restless, disturbed sleep. If at all, their worries allowed them to sleep. Before the clock struck 2 a.m., in the darkness, people emerged from the building as shadows with their backpacks and handheld bags. They moved quietly towards the main field.

And then, everyone could do nothing but wait.

People occasionally looked up at the sky, but no one could spot any helicopters. Around 3.30 a.m., after waiting for an hour and a half, a five-seater helicopter was spotted. The helicopter landed in the centre of the field amidst an ear-deafening rumble, blowing up a cloud of dust.

A group moved in a line towards the helicopter. The first lot to go had been informed in advance. The university president and his wife were among them.

The others stared at them in disbelief. It took them some time to comprehend that perhaps today was not the day they would get out of this compound.

By the time they could gulp down this harsh reality, the helicopter whizzed past and was up in the sky. They still waited, but no other chopper or Chinook came.

The group left behind was beginning to get angry and frustrated. Some of them started shouting, 'Is this some kind of a joke? Are we supposed to stand and witness their departure, wave goodbye to them and go back in silence?'

'We demand a proper explanation. Someone from here will have to answer us.'

They stood there demanding an explanation, but none came.

Slowly, the weary bodies dragged themselves back to their rooms. Heads hung in disappointment and frustration.

Even though the officers apologized and reassured everyone that the evacuation was not based on rank or position and the plan included everyone, it did not do much to calm the minds of the people waiting to be evacuated from there.

They had now spent three days waiting, and slowly, their enthusiasm dwindled and their appetites withered. There was no light-hearted banter, and no one was discussing politics or the situation outside. Cathy and Anjali usually kept quiet, reading a book they were carrying or poring over their laptop, whenever the internet connection allowed.

Nadia was busy typing away on her laptop at all times. When asked about it, she smiled and said she was working on her pending assignments. Her firm belief was that her education would still carry on. At least someone had faith amongst the others who were slowly giving up as days leaned on to evenings and evenings turned to nights.

Fawzia was spending most of her time with her son in the open. So were Zohra and her husband. The young couple could be seen walking hand in hand or sitting under a tree and chatting. Perhaps they were dreaming about their future and how life was going to be for them once they were out of this rut. Anjali saw them and smiled; she was happy that some of them still had dreams to cherish and nourish. She wished that their hope and positivity would have a rub-off effect on those who were slowly sinking into depression and hopelessness.

The officers would come intermittently to meet everyone and brief them about the news that was trickling in. The Taliban spokesperson announced that the war was over and that they would not harm anyone. They even announced that they would allow people to leave the country if they desired. Foreign media were also heard speculating that the prisoners leaving Bagram and Pul-e-Charkhi prisons would include ISIS members, and hence, the airport and other places may not be safe for civilians.

This news led to days of waking up at 2 a.m. and dragging themselves to the field for the people inside the camp. Every time a small helicopter came, it ignited some hope in everyone. The hope was soon extinguished when it left, taking only a few chosen ones with it.

6

Since she had left the university campus, Dr Cathy had hardly been her real self. She spoke less, usually kept to herself, brooded at times, was irritable, and often snapped when asked or told anything. Anjali and the rest tried to avoid her moodiness, attributing it to the current situation and maybe the impending loss of her job and source of income.

Anjali, too, was worried about not having a job anymore. However, that worry was superseded by the stress of making it out of here safely. The safety and warmth of her own house, and perhaps a tension-free, relaxed life.

For Fawzia, Nadia and Zohra, the reality was slightly different—they were planning and reshaping their life in their minds with hopes of what lay ahead of them, a life of promise. Sometimes, one could spot them talking animatedly in Dari, sharing a news clip or a video on their phone.

The bond that they seemed to have developed that night in the basement was missing, and they were just together because they belonged to the same organization, and nothing more than that. The sisterhood seemed to have withered with time.

The worry of reaching a safe place, of who would avail the helicopter first, was bothering them. The Afghans thought that the expats would be given preference, and the expats thought that perhaps the Afghans would have someone helping them internally.

The five of them were in the same room post-lunch, indulging in small chit-chat when suddenly Dr Cathy spoke, 'I have found a way out of this place and back to safety. I can discuss it with you all if you are interested in coming with me.'

Cathy looked at all of them intently, 'I completely understand if you don't want to.'

Everyone sat up, putting their book or phone away, eager to hear what she had to say.

She began, 'This is not going anywhere. They are more interested in evacuating the who's who of different organizations, and rightly so. Their lives are more valuable than ours. However, our lives are valuable too—for us, for our loved ones and our friends and families wherever they are.

'Fawzia and Zohra have dragged other lives with them and are responsible for their well-being. The way it is going here, it will take months to evacuate us. That is, if we are still alive. I don't know about you all, but for me, every day is becoming a living nightmare. I cannot eat, sleep or concentrate on anything. I keep reading the same page repeatedly, trying to comprehend its meaning. I am petrified thinking of what might happen to us. I don't see any ray of hope anywhere. We were sacrificial lambs, and nobody is going to bother about us, if we don't do it ourselves.'

Dr Cathy looked visibly angry and exhausted as she reached out for a bottle of water in her agitated state.

'I just cannot take the stress of knowing that this could be the last day that I am breathing, eating or walking around. I came to work in this place, true, I also admit that I knew I was coming to Kabul to work. But that doesn't mean that I am going to be a prisoner and just stay here at the mercy of a bunch of people who were bad planners and are now not capable of rescuing us. True, we were not their responsibility, but shouldn't they be trying to do something? My guest comes to my house, is it not my duty to see them off safely?'

She took some hurried gulps, wiped her mouth and looked at everyone for some kind of answer.

Everyone kept quiet. After a few moments of silence, Anjali spoke, 'What can we do? How are we going to get out of this place? We hear gunshots and missiles; it is not safe out there. The airport is a nightmare; people are dying by just being trampled by others, it is chaotic, and stampedes have become a regular thing.

'The security here is very tight; outside, the whole place is manned by Taliban soldiers who are merciless. We are just five women, a man and a child. We both are foreigners, easily identifiable, and belonging to another religion. We know nothing about the ins and outs of this city. We have no friends or family here to rely upon. Zohra, Nadia and others are also fleeing; their being here is a secret even from their families. Who will help us?'

Cathy nodded and replied, 'Exactly. I know all this. All these soldiers owe their allegiance to their leaders only. They will do what they are commanded to do. Someone controls them and gives them instructions. And it is this "someone" who is going to help us.'

She paused for a second as if she knew the effect her next words would have on her friends. 'I have been in contact with Shahabuddin Shuja. Yes, you heard me right. Shahabuddin.'

Everyone gasped upon hearing that name.

Shahabuddin was a notorious warlord, and in the nineties, he was responsible for killing thousands of people. He killed anyone who didn't belong to his tribe. Apart from killing, he was known for drug trafficking, human trafficking, arms dealing, and more. He was a dreaded name, and people avoided associating with his name or having anything to do with him.

It was beyond anyone's comprehension that Dr Cathy had somehow established a link with this man.

There was silence in the room; no one had anything to comment on or ask. They were still trying to soak in the news. There was only one question looming large in all their minds—how much does one compromise, or to what length can one go to fulfil their needs? Where lies the boundary, and at what point does it get obliterated? Do circumstances justify the means in pursuit of the end?

Dr Cathy realized the discomfort and knew what everyone was thinking.

'There is no other way. He is powerful, and every soldier will listen to him. He controls the most dominant and powerful tribe. In times like this, you need to be with the powerful one and not depend on those who are not even capable of arranging for a large helicopter and have complete disregard for the women they have invited into their institution.

'I followed the proper way, what did I get? A plank to sleep on and a plate of insipid pasta, with days of languishing here looming endlessly? I have had enough, just enough!

'I know Shahabuddin's nephew; we have worked together on several research projects. He is a nice, friendly guy. You may have seen him around campus, a tall, lanky, bespectacled guy named Khalid.'

She turned to Anjali, 'Do you remember him, Anjali?

'Khalid has just come back from Washington and is now in the thick of this chaos, but he will leave soon. He has promised to help us out, the five of us, if we want. He has spoken to his uncle, and his uncle has agreed. I speak to Khalid regularly and am in touch with him through text messages. He is aware of our situation, and he sympathizes with it. He has been able to convince his uncle.'

'Are you sure he can do that? There will be seven of us and not five; I cannot leave my husband behind. Fawzia won't leave her son either,' said Zohra.

Fawzia nodded her head in agreement, 'If we go, they go. Or we do not go.'

Cathy nodded. 'Yes, yes, my bad. It will be seven. I have not given them the exact head count or names. I just mentioned that there are a bunch of us from the university. We will need an SUV, a vehicle that can take eight to ten of us together. I don't think he is that interested in the number or the description of the people who are going to be with me—I was not even sure whether I would be able to convince you all to come with me.'

Cathy knew she had convinced everyone. And she knew the time for action was now.

'Okay, listen, this is what the plan is. Listen to me very carefully. First, I need to seek the permission of the commanding officer that we are going to leave on our own. There will be an initial resistance, but they cannot hold us back, especially when they are incapable of finding any alternative. I suspect that there will be some paperwork, consent forms, etc., to be signed. That is the usual protocol.

'Once we have the designated vehicle, we head straight for the airport. There is a special flight for Qatar, and Khalid will arrange seats for us. We fly to Qatar together, and after that, you find your way to your home or wherever you wish to go, understood? Of course, we need to pay for the tickets, and mind you, they are not cheap.'

Nadia and Fawzia almost spoke together, 'How much will it be? I have limited money with me.'

Their question remained unanswered.

'This sounds fairly simple, but I am guessing it is not going to be so simple,' said Anjali.

'Nothing in life is simple, my dear. A lot of coaxing, negotiation, begging, requesting and promises have already gone behind the whole exercise. It wasn't easy for me.

'It is not going to be simple going ahead, too—whether it is getting permission to leave the premises of this safe house or getting to where we have to.

'But don't forget, we came here of our own free will, and we go when we feel like. We can't be kept as prisoners. Ladies, are you with me on this?

'The situation outside is chaotic. Almost all embassy staff have been evacuated. Thousands of Afghans are rushing to the airport with the thought that they might be able to get onto a plane and leave the country. People are climbing walls, ignoring barbed wires and even throwing their babies over the boundary wall. It looks like hell on earth. Do you think someone in this situation will bother to send a helicopter to rescue a bunch of teachers? I doubt that.'

Zohra finally spoke, 'If this is the situation, do you think we will manage to get seats on the Qatar-bound flight? Will we even reach the airport? Will Khalid ensure that? Will he have someone who will get us Qatari visas?'

Everyone had their take on this, and it was followed by discussions and debates, weighing the pros and cons.

Since there were not many options left, and till now, all other arrangements had not worked, everyone agreed to take the plunge and try it out. Maybe this was the only way out. By now, they had all understood that not much help was coming for them anyway from any other quarter.

Cathy almost immediately went away to discuss it with the commander, although it was almost nine in the evening and everyone had gone back to their rooms after dinner. She was gone for a long time and came back looking exhausted. Everyone knew it would not have been a straightforward conversation. She had to give a lot of explanations and was reprimanded for getting in touch with Shahabuddin, more for letting him know about their whereabouts. Cathy was scolded for being reckless in endangering the lives of those on the compound. She apologized and had to give a written statement about her plan, which stated that she was willing to take the risk on her own accord.

The commander of the camp reached out to the university president, who had reached Doha and was there with some other members who could be potential donors to run the university. He wanted to speak to Cathy, and they had a long conversation. Cathy had to convince him that she could take responsibility for the others. The commander wanted to meet the others in her group. They spoke about their consent. Khalid was contacted, and the commander spoke to him, asking for a detailed plan. Photocopies of their passports were taken, and then everyone had to write a consent note individually. A general statement was also drafted.

The statement had to be signed by all of them. The paperwork and process continued till late at night. There were several rounds of discussion, and in every conversation, they were warned about the dangers of such an endeavour. While others kept quiet, Cathy took the lead and was adamant that this was the best possible way out for them, and ultimately, the commanding officers relented.

Once the documents had been signed and the plans discussed in detail, it was decided that the car would come around 6 a.m. when things were a bit quieter before the day broke. They were to keep their passports and bags handy.

It was decided that money would be exchanged at a pre-decided spot inside the airport, and tickets for the aircraft bound for Qatar would be given to them just before boarding the plane. They were to keep to the group, not answer any questions and let Cathy do all the talking since she had brokered the deal. Once they reached home, Cathy and Anjali would transfer the agreed amount of money to whoever was designated by Shahabuddin, through a system called 'hawala'—transactions done without any proper paperwork or receipt. Anjali and Cathy would cover for Fawzia and Nadia till they could repay the loans.

On the morning of 17 August, four days after they had come to this safe house, and two days since Kabul had fallen to the Taliban, these five women, a child, and a man left the compound in a black SUV. They were accompanied only by the driver. The car was old and unassuming, and they were glad that it was so, hoping that they would go unnoticed.

The ladies, irrespective of their origin or religion, were fully covered in an abaya, with their backpacks in hand. They once again braced themselves for a new journey towards freedom, an attempt to escape the ordeal. Some of them were murmuring prayers, seeking the blessings of the guardian angels to ensure a smooth and safe passage. They were hoping that today would be the day when their ordeal would come to an end. They were all dreaming of reclining their heads on the seats inside an aircraft, seeing the clouds floating below them, and heaving a sigh of relief.

7

On an average day, the journey from Shahr-e Naw, where the compound was, to the airport should not have taken more than nineteen minutes; at the maximum, it would take forty minutes. The route was simple: pass Shahr-e Naw to Akbar Wazir Khan, on to Azizi Plaza and then the straight road towards the airport.

Minutes passed, and they felt like long, tedious hours. Everyone was looking at the car's dashboard clock intently, but the destination was not in sight.

Cathy and Anjali were not familiar with the roads or their names. Cathy had gone to the airport twice, bundled inside a car with two soft-skin vehicles guarding the one in which she was traveling. Anjali had come only a few months back, and the road to the airport was not familiar to her at all. She did spot some blue-glassed buildings, one of which looked like a plaza or a mall, but she couldn't read the letters in Farsi.

It was when the car took a diversion and drove towards the Avesta hospital, passed the university campus of a private university near Taimani and then took a turn towards

Market Road, that Nadia muttered loudly, 'Why is he taking this diversion? This is not the route to the airport. This is a completely wrong turn towards Nooran Hospital. We are not meant to take this road. What is happening?'

Everyone looked at her in confusion. She leaned forward and asked the driver, 'Why did you take Ahmad Shah Baba Road? This doesn't go towards the airport.'

The driver kept driving and focused on the road ahead.

'Hello! I am speaking to you, could you please answer!'

Her voice became shrill as she asked the question again.

Everyone was holding their breath, the air inside the car was thick with apprehension, and the smell of sweat was mixed with fear. Even Fawzia's son, who was playing with a plastic toy, stayed still, frozen in his place.

Zohra's husband, who was sitting beside the driver, now placed his hand on his shoulder, understood the situation and politely asked, 'Nasir Jan, are you confused? Do you know the road to the airport? If you want, I can drive the vehicle, I don't mind.'

'We must hurry, this is just causing us delay, after this, the crowd will start swelling on the road to the airport, and we will be stranded,' said Zohra's husband.

The driver turned towards him, gave him a stern look and, in a low voice, let out a growl, which, when translated by others, was asking her husband to sit quietly and not to disturb him. He said he knew what he was doing and was doing exactly what he had been instructed to do.

Zohra turned towards Cathy and said in a steel-cold voice, 'I hope you realize that your plan has failed. We are knee-deep in muck, and I am sure you don't have a way out of this. You couldn't foresee this, could you? Your contacts are not helping, it seems. You have put us all in danger, including the life of this small boy. Well done! Bravo!'

No sooner had she spoken than the car came to a halt. Two men opened the door, one in the front and one beside them, and pushed them aside roughly to get into the car.

Protests didn't help; their cold stare said enough.

Fawzia let out a wail.

'Ya Allah!'

Their get-up was good enough to speak for who they were and to which side they belonged. The men were huge in stature; their muddied shirts sat tautly across their shoulders where they had placed a checkered cloth to rest their rifles. Their long hair was matted and coiled under their small skull caps. Their kohl-rimmed eyes were bloodshot and rheumy. Their shoes were dirty, carrying the dust of hilly tracks with them.

Cathy shook her head, buried her face in her hand and kept rocking to and fro, muttering to herself: 'What have I done, what have I done?'

One of the men turned towards her menacingly and told her to shut up.

Anjali, who was paralysed with dread, looked at Abhay's smiling face on her phone's screensaver and thought, *This is how you want me to come to you? This is going to be a violent one, just a prayer, make it quick and painless for me, can you do that?*

Everyone in the car knew their escape plan had gone awry. As the dust whipped up behind the speeding car, they all saw their dream of being safe at home blow away. They had nowhere to go, and Kabul had fallen.

The car meandered through lanes and by-lanes while the passengers inside sat helplessly. There was no movement; ten people in an SUV were not an easy squeeze at the best of times, and now it felt like they were helpless sardines in a can.

The car moved for another half an hour and finally stopped in front of a half-constructed building at the dead end of a narrow lane. The entire street was deserted. There was no human in sight, just a lone brown-coloured dog sniffing the sidewalk in search of food.

The two men didn't have much patience and told them to get out of the car as soon as possible. The women could feel their tobacco breath as they barked orders at them.

On any other day, this lane would be full of carts selling fruits or cheap colourful plastic mugs and low-sitting stools. It would have old matronly women bargaining or a naughty child pelting stones at a dog. But today, this place had the look of a graveyard. It was solemn and silent.

The five of them hurriedly stepped out of the car. Anjali nearly tripped as she was not used to wearing the abaya. Nadia caught her immediately and both looked at each other silently, grateful for each other's company at this time.

They were pushed inside the door and their bags were taken from them. Three flights of steps led them to another door. The walls were garishly painted in pink and had a small letter box which read something like 'Tech Comp Ltd'. *So, this was an office belonging to someone, a tech company? But where was everyone?*

They were led toward a room that resembled an office. As their eyes adjusted to the darkness, they all saw the workstations, some chairs and a water filter.

In the corner of the room was a toilet marked 'one'. The air was musty, and a thick layer of dust had settled on the furniture. The landline phone, one or two broken printers and a desktop computer were lying around, abandoned and discarded. It was evident the place had not been used for a couple of months.

The women were directed to sit on the floor. As soon as they sat, all members were asked to hand over their telephones. Anjali tried to resist this; her only balm at such a time was Abhay's pictures and voice, all in that phone.

The man, who was wearing a blue shalwar, said something rudely, and Zohra, understanding him, tore the phone away from her hand and handed it over. 'Don't resist anything, you and all of us will be in grave danger. You cannot fight these men. Do as they say. We have to obey them; we are in trouble,' she said in a hushed tone.

The phones were collected and kept in an old plastic bag bearing the logo of an obscure cloth shop in Kabul. The men kept them sitting on the floor and went away, locking the door from behind. Thankfully, they were not gagged or handcuffed.

As soon as the men left, the deathly silence engulfed them all.

Cathy broke down, 'What did I do? I shouldn't have brought you all with me; I could have faced this alone. Please forgive me, please pardon me. It is all my fault. I trusted the wrong person.'

Anjali consoled her, and the others joined in, too, 'It is not anybody's fault, you tried your best, you tried to clutch the last remaining straw, not knowing that it might sink us all. We were getting desperate. It could have been any of us.'

'Let us now think about how we can get out of this situation. I am sure there will be some scope for negotiations, maybe we can try and initiate one. Since we are kept alive and not killed by them, I have a hunch they want something from us.'

Zohra's husband volunteered to speak to the men.

'These people won't negotiate with a woman, least of all with a foreigner. Let me talk to them when they are back. Let me do this alone. You can all add your bit in English, but do not talk to them directly, it will only irk them.'

Nadia, who had kept very quiet till now, was now hugging her knees and rocking herself. Her rocking movement became more and more agitated and frequent till she resembled a woman possessed. Fawzia tried to hug her and stop her from rocking, but this only broke her more.

'I am doomed; they will soon hand me over to my husband, who will de-skin me before taking me to the Taliban. My only punishment will be to be stoned to death with thousands of onlookers cheering and urging my husband to throw the first stone.

'Maybe my brothers will join, too. I have brought shame to the family. I defied Allah's choice, no one can save me now.'

Fawzia and Zohra tried to console her even though they were feeling the grip of the paralysing fear, too.

It felt like time was standing still. Apart from the musty smell in the room and the noise of a dog barking outside, it was completely silent. Nobody knew what to do. They couldn't run outside; they were unable to call out or use their phones anymore. They just sat on the floor, resigned to their fate, tired, exhausted and scared.

The men came back after an hour. They stood in a corner and were talking among themselves in a hushed tone. Those who understood Dari could catch a few words. Cathy urged them to translate, but all they heard were words like prisoner, foreigner, money, jeep, etc. Were they planning to take them somewhere? Maybe keep them in captivity? They knew they were in a big mess, but no one had any idea which way it would go.

Anjali whispered to them, 'Breathe, breathe, take deep breaths. Let us not show them that we are scared. Let us try and be as normal as possible.' Whether people listened to her advice was anybody's guess.

Zohra's husband, Ayoub, initiated the conversation politely, leading with salaams. The discussion went on for a while with terse exchanges. Ayoub was trying to get them to tell him whose orders they were following and what was the purpose of this kidnapping. His questions made them irritable, and they shouted back at him. One of them even tried to slap him, but Ayoub apologized, 'Maafi.' His polite and apologetic voice softened them a bit.

After much negotiation and cajoling, it became evident that these people didn't have any commanders and were not working under anybody's instruction. This piece of information made the whole situation even more bizarre. What could they even want from these five women?

Ayoub realized from his conversation that they had gotten a whiff of their escape, probably from the driver of the vehicle, and were perhaps looking at making some money. They wanted fifty thousand dollars in cash and a brand-new car; an SUV would be preferred. Ayoub persuaded them to ensure that everyone remained unharmed; harming them would not get them any ransom anyway.

Ayoub realized he should discuss this with his wife's friends. Who could have thought Zohra's timid husband, who hardly spoke a word when in public, would be the one to negotiate with these thugs? He even requested them to bring some green tea and bread for the group.

Once the men left the room, Ayoub turned to Cathy, 'Dr Cathy, who did you talk to about this escape? Except for the commanding officer, who else knew about this? Who else knew that we would leave the compound at 6 a.m. besides your contacts who agreed to help you?'

Cathy denied having contacted anyone. Or maybe in all the stress, she just didn't remember who she had been in touch with.

Everyone started talking with each other, trying to figure out who could have known about their exit from the compound, which was done in secret. After a while, Cathy broke down again.

'I did. I did. How stupid of me, how could I have been so foolish! I contacted Professor Jalaluddin and told him about this plan. Do you think he leaked the information? Oh my god! I just don't believe he would do such a thing! Would he?' Her question hung in the air.

Everyone kept quiet, wondering why she had to tell someone who was not even remotely connected to the operation. It made no sense to anyone why she would do so. But despite it all, they didn't have the heart to reprimand her; their minds were too preoccupied with thinking of a way out. But at this moment, escape seemed to be a remote possibility. The whole city was in a state of chaos; there was no one to help them.

It was Ayoub who thought of the next steps. He very politely asked them to give them Cathy's phone so that they could arrange for the money. After much hesitation, they agreed. Cathy first called Khalid, the warlord's nephew. Cathy's first question was to ask if they had been involved in this—she still couldn't wrap her head around the fact that this was a random kidnapping. Khalid denied his and his uncle's involvement. However, he volunteered to negotiate on their behalf.

The phone was reconnected, and Khalid spoke to them. Shahabuddin's name seemed to have an effect. The men nodded their heads in unison as obedient students. After a conversation that left the whole group on tenterhooks, the men returned the phone to Cathy.

Khalid called back, 'This is the work of some random group. You understand the chaos that is happening. Everyone is trying to take advantage and make some quick money if they can. It is a state of complete lawlessness. They know that no one is there to catch them or punish them.

'I have spoken to them. They are, however, a bunch of proud boys, and they will not let you go just like that. They can't face their friends empty-handed. Friends who have lent them a car or opened this office for them.

'I don't know who they are and how they are connected; this information they refused to divulge. They want fifty thousand dollars in cash and a car. Not very specific about which car they want, but a new one. Banks are closed for an indefinite period, and money is not coming in anymore from the donor agencies. Can you organize something, while I try my best to do so at my end?'

Cathy thought for a while and said, 'I will get something. I created this mess, and I must get us out of this.'

After she cut the call, she thought for a moment about what to do next. Fifty thousand dollars wasn't a small amount. And where do you get a car in this chaos, let alone a new one? Khalid had done what he could; if they were to be freed, something had to be done.

The men were getting impatient. It seemed that they were in a hurry to finish things and run. Perhaps they, too, wanted to flee. Who knew what was going on in their minds?

Cathy picked up her phone and dialled a number.

She spoke to someone for a while and then turned towards them. 'It has been arranged. My student, Abdullah Ahmadzai, is on his way. He is a big businessman with lots of money. He is bringing cash and a used car; he cannot arrange for a new one at this time.

'He will take us out of this place. He is coming as soon as possible with the cash and a car,' she smiled as she addressed her group. It was a smile that they had not seen in a long time. 'I think my retirement will get postponed by five more years as I need to return the money to Abdullah now!'

Everyone heaved a sigh of relief. It was now a long wait for Mr Abdullah, hoping that he would come and make this his priority. After a little more than an hour, Abdullah came walking through the door. He was carrying a duffle bag, which he handed over to the men who were waiting in the room, smoking cigarettes.

Cathy rushed to shake hands with him, tears swelling up in her eyes. Anjali folded her hands in gratitude, too. Abdullah was polite and dismissed their gratitude by saying he just did what a true Afghan man should do for guests like his professors. Nadia and Zohra recognized him as an ex-student, a very polite and elderly student who wanted to study more to manage his business better.

Soon, all the settlement was done and they were free to go. The men snatched the bag from Abdullah's hand, took the key to the car and left the office without saying a single word. They didn't want to prolong this kidnapping game—they vanished as abruptly as they had appeared.

The drama that unfolded this morning finally came to an end. They could finally be on their way to safety.

Abdullah insisted that he would drop them back in his car at the security agency's compound.

They decided not to speak a word about this incident to anyone. By now, they were supposed to be on the flight, halfway to Doha.

They decided to go with the narrative that the flight was chock-a-block and there were no seats available, and this was the cause of their return. Abdullah agreed to go with this story, too. He had managed their ransom, but it was beyond his capability to arrange flight tickets for them. Cathy kept repeating that she would try to return Abdullah's money as soon as possible. He insisted that he was not worried about that, and his cause for worry at this moment was their safety.

As they came out, they saw a silver-coloured sedan driven by Abdullah's driver. Abdullah told his driver to go back home, and he took them in his car and dropped them off. All of them somehow squeezed themselves into the car, but no one was complaining about the sitting arrangement; they were too glad to have escaped unharmed. They now wanted to go behind the gate of the security compound, in safety.

As soon as they started walking towards their designated room, hoping that it had not been allocated to someone in the interim few hours, a guard came towards them, asking them to meet the commander in his office. Before they could reach his office, he came out in a hurry. His face looked grim and concerned.

'What happened? Couldn't you reach the airport? I hope you all are okay; the child looks tired and hungry. Is everything okay?'

As discussed earlier, Cathy started speaking, and everyone kept quiet. 'Had we known that the roads were chaotic, I wouldn't have left with them. We could hardly travel a few blocks, and our car was surrounded by rushing men and women. They were all heading towards the airport. Some of them banged our car window and tried to climb over to sit on the roof. We were so scared.

'As you rightly said, hell has broken loose. The gates to the airport are heavily guarded by Taliban soldiers. They had parked tanks along the road and were heavily armed. We tried to push the crowd and reach the airport, but we couldn't enter it. So, we decided to come back and wait for some more time, maybe a few more days for the mayhem to settle down.'

The commander was a kind man. He seemed concerned. He asked a few more questions and then told them to go to their room and rest. 'Lunch is almost finished, but I will send some snacks and tea. Do you have something to eat? I don't think any of you have eaten anything since morning. We will speak again, perhaps at dinner. I don't want to trouble you all now.'

As they reached their rooms, Fawzia insisted that her son stay with them for a while, and Zohra, too, was reluctant to let go of her husband's hand. It slowly dawned on them that today they could have been separated from each other or lost their lives; they could have been tortured and killed.

They wanted to hold on to each other and savour every precious moment. No one was around—no guard, no commander. They huddled in one room. Some toast and a few slices of cake and biscuits were given to them with two flasks of tea and coffee. They drained every drop from the flask and wiped the plates clean.

Colour started coming back to their faces, which had been pale with fear and exhaustion. While Arzoo snuggled next to his mother and dozed off to sleep, Fawzia kept kissing his sleeping face, and the others just sat around. Zohra was holding Ayoub's hand, and Nadia hugged her backpack as if it were a child. They kept repeating the incidents, trying to find a clue. They analysed the route and the exact place where those two men had climbed in. After a while, they were convinced that all this had been masterminded by the driver. They blamed Khalid for not checking on his sources, and they even blamed the warlord in a whisper that maybe he had lost control over his men. They didn't have the heart to blame Cathy, who repeatedly apologized.

Once they all left, Anjali asked Cathy a question that was bothering her.

'Cathy, if you don't mind, may I ask you something?'

Cathy looked at Anjali, it was almost as if she knew what the question would be. She was embarrassed about the failure and the fact that she had told Jalaluddin about their plan to leave for Doha.

'Why did you tell Jalaluddin about our escape when he was in no way involved in this? Do you think he was responsible for our abduction?'

Cathy looked visibly nervous. She cleared her throat and, after much hesitation, replied, 'I am so sorry, Anjali. I know I caused everyone a lot of trauma. I was blinded by jealousy.'

Anjali was confused. It didn't make sense to her to attach this emotion to Cathy.

'It was for you, Anjali! I have liked Jalaluddin since the time I joined this university. He is polite and respectful and seems to be a kind-hearted man, which is rare these days. I know he is very religious, and I have often seen him praying during meetings.

'When he started showering all his attention on you, I got very jealous. I couldn't take it. He seemed to like you and was willing to go to great lengths to help you; to him, you were a damsel in distress. I was burning with envy.

'I saw that initially, you had apathy towards him. But slowly, maybe, and I could be wrong, but I thought that you had started indulging him. Since we came here, I have seen you talking to him a couple of times. I wanted to draw his attention and thought that if I confided in him, he would soften towards me.'

She shrugged helplessly, 'I am so very foolish. I still crave the company of a man. Two horrific incidents have not taught me a lesson. I don't know if he is the one who informed others. I don't see any reason as to why he should do that, but I am genuinely sorry. Please, can you forgive me?'

Saying this, she took Anjali's hands in hers and looked at her face with eyes full of remorse.

Anjali shook her head. 'Cathy, I don't know what to say. Never once did I think you had any feelings for him. Not even when I came to your room on campus to speak to you about his behaviour toward me. Yes, I did contact him a couple of times, rather it was he who enquired about my well-being, but I think it was just out of politeness.

'I am not quite sure he is a good man or a bad man. All I know is that he is polite and, yes, you are right, respectful, and I admire that quality in every human being. You needn't have been jealous. He is nothing more than a colleague. I cannot develop romantic feelings towards someone whom I have barely met. Besides, I still don't have the mental space for it yet. It has always been Abhay for me, and even now, I keep talking to him. I just wish you had asked me once.'

Anjali sighed. She was very tired, both physically and mentally exhausted. Both kept quiet and, ultimately, Anjali went out to walk around in the fields; a bit of fresh air would be good for her weary and heavy heart.

As she left the room, Cathy sat on the bed, her head hung in shame.

The closeness that had developed between them on the campus seemed to have developed cracks. A breach of trust, the impending danger and the uncertainty of the future had frayed this relationship, perhaps permanently.

Part V

AKHERIN KOSHISH: THE FINAL ATTEMPT

8

The situation continued to worsen. Markets were hardly operational; if people were seen on the roads, they were either fleeing to safety or were those who had come to Kabul trying to escape impending arrest from the Taliban. Jalal continued sending messages, and then, on the fourth day after breakfast, he called, concerned about Anjali's well-being.

'I had meant to call you; I wanted to hear your voice every day. I can't sleep at night knowing that you are outside in this mayhem. The city is in such a chaotic state. Are you alright? Are you getting enough sleep and rest? Do you still want to reconsider your decision not to come and stay with us at our house? I could easily pick you up. I know you won't be able to cross the highway in front of our house. I know about your phobia of crossing roads. If you have to, I will hold your hand tightly. I am here to protect you from all harm, always.'

Anjali allowed him to talk; she just didn't have the energy to stop him. The world outside was filled with death and decline, and someone caring for her felt comforting. She admonished herself for doing so, but carried the conversation on for a long time.

Life was dragging its feet in the compound. There was not much activity apart from a few people strolling around, some trying to pet the security dogs or volunteering to take them for a walk. Only twenty of them remained. Some were airlifted, some managed to go to the airport and secure a ticket and some had friends in the city who came to take them to their house.

Those who remained wanted to be involved in some activities instead of sitting idly in a room. They went down to the kitchen to help those who were working there to chop or dress a salad or stir the soup. This was done as a gesture of kindness, gratitude or to ward off the sheer boredom of having nothing to do the whole day.

Fawzia could now keep her son with her and could be seen feeding him in the canteen; she looked happy to be united with him. Zohra and her husband were still housed separately, but one could see them walking hand in hand on the campus or eating their meals together, lost in their world of dreaming and planning.

Nadia still picked up her switched-off mobile and glanced nervously around her. At times, she was seen staring at the gate, her large green eyes seeing her husband walking through the gate and dragging her out by her hair. On such occasions, when her imagination got the best of her, her face would become pale and she would be seen trembling. She would often just sit on the ground in the compound, trying to overcome her fear. As for Cathy and Anjali, the betrayal had drawn a line between them, which made this waiting even more excruciating.

If one looked closely, one could find the signs of tiredness on everyone's face. One could see the clear signs of dark circles, lines of worry furrowed and etched on the forehead, wispy, unkempt hair, a wrinkled shirt that needed changing or a jacket that had lost its lustre with dirt settling on it. They ate meagrely now, always conscious of the fact that the rations were going to last only for a month.

The people at the compound were trying to ensure that everyone was kept as comfortable as possible while surrounded by a city in chaos. The camp was cautious of letting in unknown vendors from the market, and supplies were not coming in via Bagram airport.

The news was getting more depressing by the day. People were chasing taxiing flights; some even climbed onto their wings and were thrown to the ground when they started flying. The crowd was uncontrollable, and even the military was unable to check the flow; everyone in this city and beyond the city was trying to escape from the country.

Some of them who had been given valid papers were made to sit on the floor of a military evacuation flight in utmost discomfort, holding their belongings and babies close to their laps. Those who had been fortunate enough to reach home safely tweeted as to how undignified their journey had been; they were mishandled, tugged at and pushed around at the airport like cattle being ferried.

As hope was dwindling on the campus, an emergency meeting was called in the canteen just after lunch. The commander in charge came to address all those who were gathered about the situation outside the walls.

'There are killings and fights almost in every corner of the city. People have lost trust in each other. Everyone wants to leave the city and move to another country, especially the US or Germany. Bribery and the exchange of money are rampant just to secure a visa or a seat in a plane bound for the US.

'Several car bombs have been detonated across the country, killing people or injuring them. The Taliban had already started arresting people who had served the former government or worked closely with the American forces, terming them as traitors of the country and of the Afghan people.

'This is worse than a war zone, and I have served in many. There, at least, we knew the opponents and their hideouts; we knew our targets. We had plenty of ammunition to flush them out. We were not hiding as we are doing now; hiding and waiting to be cornered, pushed against the wall and killed eventually.

'I am frustrated, and I understand the frustration that you must be undergoing. We are cut off from the rest of the world, silently waiting for what is yet to come. I am sorry, I cannot paint a picture of hope any longer.'

He looked around at the motley crew assembled, and he could feel the rising terror as he gave the news to them.

'No flights are going in or out. This is an apocalypse. I am not sure how and when this is going to end.

'I am in touch with the US and Canadian governments. They are assuring me that they are with us, but how, I am not sure. We are gradually running out of rations; our electricity and water supply can be cut at any moment. It is a dire situation.'

He took a deep sigh. 'I urge everyone to keep the faith. I am sure there will be a way out for all of us, and very soon we will be with our loving family, away from all this. Let us pray for safer and more beautiful days ahead.' Saying this, the commander folded his hands and remained silent for a minute or so, perhaps muttering a prayer in his mind.

The entire hall remained silent, even the pet cat who always lurked around happily forgot to purr.

As soon as the commander left the dining hall, pandemonium broke loose: heated discussions, the shuffling of feet, the banging of tables in exasperation, the vigorous stirring of tea or coffee and the clatter of utensils. Everyone was speaking all at once. Everyone was busy discussing the outcome, planning a way out and trying on their mobiles to contact someone influential whom they once knew and maybe could help them to escape.

As everyone was about to leave the canteen, Pervez came running towards the five women from the university. He was panting and his face was flushed. 'Salaam, Mr Jalal has come to meet you all. He is with other colleagues. He was speaking to them. Could you come towards the hall?'

Anjali exclaimed without much thought, 'Jalal! What is he doing here? Who allowed him? Why is he allowed to come? He never told me that he was coming here, it's very dangerous for him to roam around like this, is he not scared for his life?'

Before Cathy could control herself, she blurted out, 'Ah! The pull! The concern for each other! Such sweetness. Let's go and figure out why he is here.'

Others who didn't understand the sarcasm were baffled and looked at each other.

Very soon, towering above the others, Jalal was there, smiling at them. He handed over a bag of dry fruits to Fawzia and said something in Dari.

Then he turned towards them and said, 'I am not sure what you are eating, hence, I thought I would bring a handful of dry fruits so that you all can share. Most of the shops are closed, and the markets are not functioning.'

Saying this, he started his usual polite conversation, asking about everyone's well-being and their plans. He elaborated on the situation outside and even showed some of the pictures he had taken of the roads of fleeing families.

Zohra's husband started asking him for details, and half the conversation was in Dari. Cathy hardly spoke to him, but noticed Jalal kept looking at Anjali, who, by now, was all too aware of those smiles and nods. They were standing and talking for a while when Jalal asked to take his leave. But before he left, he turned towards Anjali and said, 'Dr Anjali, may I have a word with you in private, if you don't mind?'

Anjali couldn't help but notice the smirk on Dr Cathy's face. Her face flushed with embarrassment, she looked down and stared at her toes, visibly shy about the situation. She mumbled a half-hearted yes and followed Jalal, who by now had slowed his pace to match her footsteps.

'Where are we going? Can we not have the conversation here? I mean in the canteen. I could offer you a cup of tea, perhaps?'

Jalal turned around with a chuckle, adding, 'This is a safe area, don't worry, there are guards all around you. Even if I wanted to kidnap you, which I desperately want to do, I can't. I just thought that I owed you some explanation, and maybe I can try and wipe that baffled look from your face. By the way, if you keep blushing like this, I will have to ask the commander to give me a room here. I won't be able to go back.' Saying this, he smiled, throwing his arms in the air.

Anjali couldn't help but think, whatever life this man leads, he surely knows the art of making a woman feel special.

They walked silently for a while and came to the ground where there were some artificial mounds made to train the force in combat games. He sat on one of them. Seeing that Anjali was finding it difficult to climb up, he put out his hand and, in one firm pull, pulled her to the top of the hill. Anjali flushed with the touch of his hand but kept quiet. He dusted a place beside him and gestured for her to sit.

'Look how gorgeous you look, so beautiful! With those eyes, a whole city can get immersed in it. I want to keep looking at you. I often imagine a cozy room where both of us are watching a cartoon, perhaps with a bowl of popcorn, away from all this chaos and humdrum. Do you imagine such a life, ever?

'I know you must be wondering why I have been giving special attention to you. You caught my attention the day you walked into the very first meeting. You are embarrassed, and I can understand, it is written all over your face. I still remember you looked so gorgeous, those lovely brown long tresses, the shimmering earrings hanging off your ears and your lovely Indian dress. I was mesmerized. You were breathtakingly beautiful.

'Now that I know time is less and I don't know whether we will meet again, I gathered my courage. I don't know why, but I feel I know you. As a Muslim, I don't believe in rebirth, or else that would be my explanation. It seems I have seen you somewhere, could be in my dreams, what do you think?' he added with his loud, wholehearted laughter.

Anjali was confused. *Was he joking, or did he mean what he was saying?*

Anjali almost whispered, 'What do you want from me? I am a widow, much older than you, and from a different country, culture and religion. I am not used to this kind of conversation. I led a life where I struggled with illness, survival and losing hope every minute, till I lost everything, finally. I am here as I need to work, also for my survival and to be able to become self-sufficient.'

'I know, I know all about you. You need not explain, and there is nothing that I want but to be in touch with you and know about your well-being. Talk to you occasionally, that's all. Is that a crime? Am I going to be punished? I just don't want to lose you in the crowd. You are very precious, at least to me,' said Jalal.

Anjali kept silent; she didn't know how to react. After Abhay left, she had just pushed these sentiments down and didn't allow them to surface. She was trying to find a suitable answer while Jalal looked at her expectantly.

Then, very softly, she said, 'All right, we will be friends and nothing more. I will keep in touch with you as and when I can. Are you going to be in Afghanistan?'

He looked at her softly and said, 'No, I will move back to the US. It is just that I don't want to leave my family behind. They are my responsibility. I promised my mother. I need to figure out how this goes, but my mind is now at rest that you have promised to be in touch and be my friend.

'Wait, there is something that I got for you,' he put his hand in his tunic; he was wearing a light-coloured Afghan shalwar and not his usual shirt and trousers. He fished out two packets of chocolate. 'I have often seen you nibbling them, they used to be kept on your office table. Shops have stopped stocking foreign brands. I could only get two for you.'

She took them politely from his hand as his finger brushed against her lightly; she then got up to go. He understood and followed her while nearing the house that housed her temporarily. He said, 'I am not too sure when I can come back again. I had to pull quite a few strings, give an appropriate explanation for my visit, whereas my sole purpose was to see you.

'I may be going off to the US sooner than you can imagine, but please do keep in touch. I wish you were with me in my house, and I could travel to India to drop you off at your doorstep, but that can't be, so please be safe.'

Anjali tried to hurry away. She knew what was coming next, but she lowered her head and walked away briskly as she heard him saying once more, 'Look after yourself for my sake, please, won't you? You don't know how precious you are to me. If the world is against you, if you ever feel abandoned, remember I am there with you, always with you. I will always be there even if you throw me away.'

She just nodded and hurried away. The heartfelt words had thrown her off. She needed to control her tears, which seemed to be swelling up from nowhere. She could no longer find appropriate words for these situations; she got overwhelmed and didn't want to reveal her emotions to a man she knew she might never meet again.

She hurried up the stairs, knowing that she needed to control her feelings even before she reached the door, as there would be curious onlookers and questions to be answered. Most of all, she dreaded the look on Cathy's face. She decided to spend some time alone with a cup of tea in the dining hall, trying to get her emotions under control.

9

What is wrong? What is right? How should one behave, what is the norm and who has the answer? Are we to follow what our culture dictates to us, turning a blind eye towards our feelings and completely shutting them down when they try to swell up in our minds?

Are we going to pretend that we are untouched by sentiments like love and go about our way as if nothing ever happened? Build a wall around us and even inside us, and try and freeze ourselves to the core?

These and many such questions bothered Anjali after she met Jalal. A small part of her told her that she liked the attention; rather, she enjoyed it. His caring self, Cathy's jealousy, the text messages, the undulation and the quiver in his voice when he spoke to her. His 'Hey', which was soft with a musical lilt, now and then, when he asked, 'How are you feeling today?' or 'You forgot me and never reverted?'

Perhaps all this was wrong.

The timing was wrong.

Being a widow and indulging in such banter was wrong.

Encouraging someone way younger than her was wrong.

Then why did everything feel right and perfect?

There was a battle that was waging outside the camp gate. There was another battle waging in her mind.

Every morning at 4 a.m., she, too, dragged herself to the helicopter grounds with her suitcase, waiting for a rescue helicopter. But none came. It seemed that people were now used to this morning's regime and its futility.

While Dr Anjali did so, wasn't a part of her mind telling her to let the helicopter not come?

Let her not leave Kabul.

Let her be with Jalal, climbing endless steps to a house on the rugged mountain. Let her recline on a rug and sip hot green tea while he breaks bread and passes a tiny portion to her.

Let her dream again and feel protected by someone close to her. To have his large arms wrapped around her while she nestles close to him, feeling his heart beating against her cheeks.

The next moment, she knew that was not what was going to be, ever. No rug, no tea, no warmth; just a cold, barren morning staring hard at her.

There are times when having adequate food, water, shelter and apparent freedom is not enough. As humans, we all want that stability, that certainty in life that will motivate us to keep going, and the people in the camp just wanted that. They no longer cared for grilled kebabs, pulao or that extra tin of baked beans. They no longer cared for the vast expanse of green fields in front of them to roam around.

They were not bothered by the safety of the walls and barricades around them; they just wanted to know how things were going to be and what was in store for them. They were becoming restless, very restless, and it was a cause of concern among the security in charge and commanders.

Nadia was petrified; she even dialled her brother's number once from someone else's phone and heard his voice, but didn't muster up the courage to speak. Zohra was tired of motivating her husband and spinning endless tales of how beautiful life would be if they managed to escape and reach Canada. A deafening silence descended between them. His eyes had accusations, and hers had tiredness and exhaustion in them. Cathy's eyebrows were knitted in constant frowns. She was mincing her sentences; she was plotting, measuring and evaluating her situation, and it seemed her mind was planning ways to secure her future.

Fawzia's son couldn't understand why he was not allowed to be with his grandparents and why he couldn't go to school anymore. He kept trailing behind his mother and looked depressed. No amount of humour would make him smile, and people were exhausted and didn't want to carry on playing with him. One would see him picking gravel on the sidewalk, walking around aimlessly or chasing some insect or a bird.

Anjali wanted this situation to end; she, too, was worried about having a job, rebuilding her financial situation and being in the safety of her apartment amidst the memories of Abhay scattered all over the place. All she wanted was to pull the blanket over her and sleep on her bed, the blanket that both she and Abhay shared. If no comfort can be sought in someone else's arms, then it is better to go back to the old and familiar, which is what she decided to do.

She just didn't want to think of all that her mind implored her to think, to replay the moments of Jalal talking to her in a loop, in her mind. The touch of his hand or his soft voice disturbed her. She felt she was betraying her husband's memories for something delusional, something so impermanent.

But somewhere she knew, this indecision could cost her dearly, even her life, if she didn't escape Kabul in time. That's when she dialled the number of Squadron Leader Varma. He was the first person from the Indian embassy who had contacted her when she came to Kabul and registered her whereabouts with the embassy. He answered her call immediately and was glad to find her safe.

The situation wasn't much better there.

'You know about the dam that is being constructed? We have a lot of engineers stuck there and their families, too. We have been coordinating with our other offices in Kandahar and Herat and trying to get them to Kabul. It is not an easy task.

'I am sorry that I couldn't reach you or contact you. I should have, you are our responsibility, too. I am sorry; it was neglect on our part.'

Anjali felt bad for the man on the other side, who sounded burdened. 'It is absolutely fine. I know that you must be rescuing thousands of those already stranded, and it is the responsibility of our government. I came here on my own, not at the behest of my government. Sadly, the university is not taking any responsibility. I feel so abandoned. You know, all my belongings are also kept there on the campus. It must have been looted by now. Some of those things were precious to me, handpicked by Abhay.'

'I am sure that Mr Abhay, wherever he is, is more interested in your well-being and safety, and not those things that you both so lovingly gathered. I cannot fully understand your sentiments, but I sympathize with you and can maybe try and feel what you are going through.

'Can you reach the embassy? Or at least somewhere nearby? We don't have too many vehicles, or else I would have reached you. We should have more rescue flights soon.'

'I am going to try my best. I want nothing more than to reach home safely. This is so tiring and exhausting. I think I have not slept for a while. I just wanted to go and be with my mother, in my own house and away from all this chaos,' Anjali replied.

They chatted for a while, and Squadron Leader Varma briefed Dr Anjali about the security situation and the process of taking people back to India.

By the end of the conversation, Anjali knew that nothing was more important to her than going back home, away from the mayhem and chaos. She knew that she needed to work towards it and reach the people of her own country, somehow. Anyhow.

◈

Cathy, who was getting restless like the others, called Abdullah for a way out. She had not contacted Abdullah since the kidnapping incident. That evening, they were gathered in the same room when she called him.

'Dr Sahiba, maybe if you ask for the moon, I can try and get you there, but tickets to fly out of Kabul are next to impossible.

I, too, am waiting in line to take my family elsewhere. Perhaps to Dubai, where I have an office.'

Cathy urged him to arrange tickets to anywhere, even to Doha. But he refused. 'Tickets are not being sold in the open market—it is now controlled by a few, and they are selling them for exorbitant prices. Even if you are prepared to give the quoted amount, seats are limited and are already booked for those who can wield their influence. No way can I procure tickets to Doha; I am so sorry.'

After some hesitation, and because Cathy refused to give up, he suggested another way.

'I can only suggest something, and the suggestion is not going to be a pleasant proposition, but rather a difficult one. My business hasn't stopped, and my trucks still move to Pakistan via the Torkham border. I know those people at the checkpoints, the previous regime and the newly appointed ones.

'I can try and smuggle you and take you to Pakistan. You are free to move from there. It is not going to be easy, it will be very risky, but that is the only option I can presently offer.'

Cathy sat up from her half-propped position and kept the pillow aside. Her mind raced. This wasn't a solution she wanted. It was risky, and as unpredictable as it could get. Everyone knew the borders between Afghanistan and Pakistan were rife with danger. But her practical nature didn't want to slam the door on this idea when every other door was shut on her.

'Abdullah, our backs are against the wall. What could be riskier than waiting for your death and seeing it approaching? Tell me more. You are on speaker, and we have everyone in this room except Fawzia's son, who is playing with Pervez outside.'

'Dr Sahiba, this is simple yet very complex. I have a consignment of nuts, saffron and other products reaching Pakistan in a few days. Two of my trucks are scheduled to cross the border. I can take you all to the border crossing and ensure you a space in those trucks. Some corrupt officials on both sides of the border need to be bribed adequately, and I will do that.

'While most of the time it all works seamlessly, there may be times when we meet an honest officer who wants to do all kinds of due diligence, and that is when things go out of hand. Hopefully, we won't encounter such a situation. Bear in mind, the ride is not a pleasant one, the truck, the loaded goods, the road, nothing is going to be pleasant.

'Think about it and let me know.' And he cut the call.

Cathy turned towards the others. 'So? What do you think? I feel that it is the only possible option left for us now. I cannot think of any other alternative.'

Anjali shook her head. 'I cannot go to Pakistan; I don't have a valid visa. I don't want to be there illegally and languish in jail. This is too dangerous. I have contacted my embassy and would rather go home with them.'

Cathy smirked, shrugged her shoulders and said, 'If that is what you want, then it is okay. What about the others?'

Zohra didn't look very convinced either. 'I am worried that this might be another failed attempt. This will cost us money; our money is limited, and we cannot afford to lose it in failed attempts. I am not even sure it will work. What about Arzoo? He is just a little boy. Will it be possible for him to undertake this journey? It would be physically very exhausting.'

No one could come to a decision, but they wanted to escape and find a way out of this situation, which didn't seem to be heading anywhere. The apprehension of getting caught, punished and humiliated was overwhelming, yet no one could come to a conclusion. Very soon, they started to stifle yawns, weary with the futility of the situation, and decided to think afresh in the morning.

Everyone urged Dr Anjali to be with them, but she was adamant; she didn't want to be a part of this adventure anymore. She just wanted to be in the Indian embassy, where rescuing her would be the responsibility of her countrymen. Cathy, after much persuasion, gave up and promised to speak to Abdullah to arrange for a car to take her to the embassy.

The lights were switched off, and everyone went into a sleep tinged with worry and indecision. They knew they had to make a decision quickly if they hoped to reach safety soon.

Close to midnight, the sirens started blaring through the campus. The noise was ear-deafening. It lasted for a few seconds, and what followed was a spine-chilling announcement that made everyone freeze.

The commander's loud and clear voice boomed through the personal announcement system.

'Ladies and gentlemen, we have only a few minutes in our hands before we face the worst nightmare of our lives: the Taliban is advancing in four open vehicles and is heading straight to the camp.

'Please bring your suitcase and leave it next to the staircase, all your precious belongings too. We will try to broker a deal. Switch off the lights in your room and hide under your bed.

Remember to put your phone on silent mode. If they confront you, don't try to resist but give yourself up. Fighting is futile. Non-resistance may save your life.'

This was the worst possible situation that everyone avoided imagining, although it was very much on their mind. This was inevitable and had only been stalled for some time. For a fraction of a second, it felt like a bad dream.

The second and repeated announcement jolted them from their stupor, and everyone dragged their small suitcase, duffle bag and other belongings out.

Nadia didn't want to part with her money, so she stuffed it inside her shirt. Seeing her, the others did the same. Cathy and Anjali went downstairs and hurriedly deposited their suitcase at the entrance near the base of the staircase, where a few were already piled up.

The young soldiers were busy running with them and stacking them near the gate. Cathy and Anjali came back to the room, switched off the light and crouched under their beds. In the darkness, Anjali looked at her screensaver once again, Abhay's smiling face.

Moments passed without any noise from anywhere. Suddenly, they heard the clanging of the big iron gate, followed by loud voices. Then, suddenly, a few bullets were fired, and everyone froze where they were.

It seemed that complete silence had enveloped the camp, and all that one could hear was the shallow breathing of scared souls. The whole place resembled hell. Nadia, in her fear, had passed urine and was moaning under her breath.

The stench of urine, the heat of the August month and the fans being switched off were becoming unbearable, yet they were all hiding under their beds as if the bed was their sole protector and would shield them from evil men and their guns.

Anjali, who had given up on praying after her husband's death, was now murmuring the sacred hymn of lord Hanuman, whom she knew was the protector of all. Cathy crossed her heart several times and Nadia recited verses of protection from the Quran. Everyone was praying to their deities or God for protection and to help them pass through this hard time.

Time was taking its own pace to tide over, prolonging the agony and the apprehension. Holding their breath and crouching under the bed was the only way to protect themselves.

10

Nobody had a clue how long they had been hiding under the bed. It was getting difficult to breathe. The room was hot. Crouching under the bed with almost no air or light was torturous.

Minutes passed and became hours. There was a din downstairs, a hurried running sound, the clanging of metals, the sound of a vehicle, the screeching of tires. Even that became silent after a while.

Suddenly, the lights were switched on, and the fans started moving slowly and lethargically in a languid whirling. Anjali, Nadia and Cathy dragged themselves out from under the bed. It wasn't an easy task, at least for the two of them, as age was catching up fast and was showing signs on their knees, elbows and other painful joints. They twisted and turned themselves to shake off the stiffness and the pain that had slowly crept up their numb limbs. They flopped themselves on the bed with a sigh, mopping their foreheads and tucking a few unruly hair strands behind their ears.

Energy had seeped out of them, and they simply didn't have the energy to find out what happened and what didn't. Nadia volunteered to go and find out what had happened.

Both Anjali and Cathy had not spoken much after Jalaluddin visited the camp the other day. Even today both lay down on their bed facing the wall, weary of the situation and each other's company.

Nadia came back all flustered with Zohra and Fawzia trailing behind.

'They came in huge jeeps, probably bullet-proof ones. There must have been around twelve of them, and all were heavily armed with machine guns, grenades and even knives. They looked ferocious and were ready to kill at the order of their commander.

'I heard he is a big leader and a dreaded one of the Al-Kanni group. You heard about them, right? They control half the force. They demanded to enter the hostels and wanted to kill us all. Allah! What would have happened?' Nadia shuddered, hugged her knees and sat silent for a few seconds. Everyone sat silently, perhaps trying to imagine the worst predicament that could have befallen them a few minutes ago.

Nadia resumed speaking, 'There were negotiations; they demanded money. They took all our belongings and loaded each suitcase in their huge jeeps. I heard there was an exchange of cash. Someone told me it was over a hundred thousand dollars in cash and a huge shipping container filled with guns and ammunition which they will take tonight after they bring a trailer.'

'Those shiny steel ones near the training field. You have seen those, haven't you? The commander sounded upset; he would speak to all of us at breakfast. There is no lining up for the helicopters tomorrow morning. It is just too dangerous. I guess there is nothing left to exchange apart from our lives.'

Anjali patted Nadia, 'You are a very brave girl, you got us all the information. I think there is not much we can do tonight. Let us rest and pray that tomorrow is better than today and that we all reach home safely. I am not sure how much we can sleep; sleep is becoming elusive but let us at least close our eyes and rest our bodies. We need to calm our senses as much as we can.'

They lingered in the room for a while, talking and discussing the same issue repeatedly till they started stifling yawns and slowly retired to their respective beds. Uncertainty covered them and lulled them to a restless sleep, and the entire camp waited for some more danger to unfold in the night.

The commander had a sleepless night, one could not help but notice the red-rimmed eyes and dark circles, his dishevelled hair and his crumpled shirt. His neatness and his proud upright stance had disappeared overnight, and he looked like a ghost of his former self.

The next morning, no one was in the mood to enjoy their breakfast. There was some kind of hushed eerie silence in the once-animated dining hall.

The commander cleared his throat and started talking to the crowd.

'We have been compromised. We have been breached, and we are no longer safe. They have all the information, how many of you are here, from where, what age group, everything. I did what I could do to keep them away from us.

'I bartered. I exchanged. I negotiated and gave all that had some kind of material value. I have nothing more to give but offer us, and that I will not do till I am alive.

'I cannot keep you safe anymore. You are free to look after yourself and do whatever you think is good for you. You are free to leave the camp; you don't need to consult me or ask my permission … not anymore.' Saying this he left the room, head hanging as if he had lost the last battle of his life.

Everyone felt sorry for him, but also knew they had to figure out a way now. All on their own.

The five women from the university gathered around and discussed the situation for a while. Two of their male colleagues were leaving that afternoon and taking refuge in the house of their local counterparts.

Another one had contacted his ex-student and would stay with him for the time being. It seemed they had already started carving out a way for themselves. The women went back to their room to discuss this and decide their course of action.

Anjali, while climbing the steps to their room, decided that she needed to reach the Indian embassy at the earliest; she didn't want to risk another night of being here; the Taliban knew their location now. Nothing was stopping them from coming back to finish what they couldn't do then.

She needed a safe vehicle with a driver who would manoeuvre the roads and take her safely to the embassy. She decided to discuss it with the commander of the camp.

Others were not feeling safe either. They, too, wanted to leave, and the only option available to them was the one suggested by Abdullah. To hide in his trucks and cross the border to Pakistan. They all agreed to follow what Cathy had decided.

Cathy connected with Abdullah, who promised to reach them by the afternoon to discuss an escape route. The morning was spent speculating various possibilities and gathering information from some local colleagues who were still in Kabul.

Abdullah arrived just after lunch and sat down in the canteen with a cup of coffee to discuss a possible escape route. He kept a pen and paper and soon started drawing a map.

'We need to reach the Torkham border. Those who are Afghans, you all are familiar with this border crossing. For the others, it is the border that connects Afghanistan to Pakistan. At this point, the checkpoints are manned by the Taliban, and it is not going to be easy to bypass them. We shall try our best.'

Cathy interrupted, 'How do we reach Torkham? Is it not going to be far from here, and the roads are dangerous, as I have gathered.'

'Yes, it is going to be difficult. The roads are chaotic, and no one knows what is waiting for us at the end of the road, but this is a chance you need to take. Are you willing to do that?'

Saying this, Abdullah looked at everyone, as if scanning their faces for a suitable answer. He was a cautious man, and he didn't want to get caught on the wrong foot; taking responsibility for so many women and a child was risky.

Cathy said, 'Let's discuss it once more. Just give us ten minutes, and in the meantime, let me get you a cup of coffee and you rest for a while.'

'Sure, make it a cup of tea, please! We Afghans are not that fond of coffee, and I just swallowed one,' chuckled Abdullah.

Cathy ushered the entire group to another table, and everyone followed her. Anjali, however, wanted to stay back and talk to Abdullah about her arrangements.

Cathy threw her hand in the air in a sheer gesture of displeasure and perhaps a bit of anger, but Anjali decided to ignore it. She was not bound to listen to her senior colleague now. Not when they were out on the streets, looking for desperate measures to save themselves.

Anjali sat down in front of Abdullah; she felt like crying. She was scared for her life and what lay ahead of her. She started speaking to Abdullah, who looked up at her with sympathetic eyes.

'I am sorry, Abdullah, for troubling you. I never had the opportunity to teach you or supervise your work. I heard a lot about you from various colleagues and staff, and everyone said that you are a kind man.

'You operate businesses in many countries, and you know the reality between my country and that of my neighbouring country. I just don't feel safe about travelling there illegally without proper documents. I might be jailed as a trespasser. I have heard many such horrific stories of people who remained in jail for years, and no amount of negotiation helped. I am not willing to take this risk.'

Abdullah nodded in agreement and asked, 'You are right, this can happen. Do you have any other plans in mind? Do you want to continue staying here till things get a bit normal? I heard you have some very good friends.'

Anjali blushed a bit, she knew that Abdullah was hinting at Jalal. News travelled faster than air in this land, it seemed.

She nodded her head and said, 'No, I don't want to stay here. I don't know what you heard, but again, no, I don't have any friends here. I want to reach the Indian embassy. I have already spoken to them. They have a rescue flight, and I can go back home.'

'Oh! That would be great. That is not a problem at all. When do you want to leave? I can drive you down and see to it that you are inside the gate of your embassy. You should have told me earlier. This will be the easiest thing to do.'

Anjali was grateful. She folded her hands and said, 'If it is possible, maybe today. I don't want to miss the rescue flight. Let me make a call to the embassy, and then I can go and pick up whatever is left of my belongings.'

Abdullah agreed and said he would wait for her.

While the others were moving towards the table that seated Abdullah, Anjali quickly went upstairs. The curious onlookers had questions written on their faces, but she ignored them.

She dialled Squadron Leader Varma's number as she began to move toward her room. She told him about her plan to reach the embassy that day itself. Varma agreed immediately and said that he would be at the gate when she reached it.

All she needed to do was to pick up her backpack. Before leaving, she looked at the room one more time. The room that had housed her in times of dire need. She thanked the universe. A thought crossed her mind to inform Jalal, but she refrained. Could he be trusted? What was the need to inform him of her every move?

Cathy and the others were now engaged in a deep conversation with Abdullah.

He explained the route again. 'We need to first reach Jalalabad, which on a normal day would take us two hours and not more than three hundred afghani. You need to travel in a taxi. I cannot bring my car as I will be questioned, especially with so many women in my car.

'But before that, I needed to get you a false visa; many expired visas are being recycled. The cost used to be around three hundred and fifty American dollars, but that was earlier; I will try to negotiate hard. Then from Jalalabad to Torkham. The road to Jalalabad is a difficult one, it's mountainous and dangerous.'

Ayoub commented, 'Yes, we Afghans know that. We have been there.'

'From Jalalabad to Torkham, you will be in my truck, and you will be hidden amongst my goods. All this can be worked out but first let me get hold of the visas. The name is not a problem. Half of the security guards can't read, but the description must match, especially that of the child and Ayoub who will be without a burqa.'

There were some more questions. Some more clarity was sought about the route, cost and details of the stay en route to Peshawar.

Abdullah tried to furnish them with as much information as possible while he waited for Anjali.

When Anjali came in with her backpack, everyone knew she was leaving. Nadia rushed to hug her, and so did the others. The last of them was Cathy.

'It is always a man, isn't it? I was not very polite to you earlier. I was desperate and worried and jealous, but you were wonderfully patient and always smiling. Perhaps you should have left earlier and gone to your embassy. Do keep in touch with us, I am sure we will meet again—and maybe online very soon.'

As Anjali started walking towards the gate, she felt a pang of sadness and guilt for abandoning her colleagues and mainly Arzoo, who kept waving at her. She looked back as the gate was closed. They were still standing in a group together. Goodbyes were always the hardest and the most painful.

Anjali got into the car and heaved a sigh. Abdullah understood and decided not to interrupt her thoughts while he started backing the car before it hit the road.

Anjali decided to concentrate on the road and left her thoughts behind in the camp where they originated and now died a slow death. Life must go on, some with the sheer thought of progress and with promises of a better tomorrow.

She kept repeating to herself in her mind, 'Everything is impermanent', and braced herself for the onward journey with just one thought overwhelming her mind: to reach home safely.

11

Abdullah drove her through lanes and by-lanes, carefully avoiding the road junctions where a tank or military vehicles had been parked. All around them were young men in traditional wear, skullcaps or turbans, sporting long hair.

They all had a Kalashnikov or some kind of ammunition with them. They had hardened jaws and looked intimidating. It was clear that they meant business. They would not allow even a bird to fly unnoticed, unquestioned or unsearched, and only when they were satisfied would they allow safe passage.

Driving a car with an Indian Hindu woman sitting beside you, not covered, not your relation, trying to escape, was not at all a good situation. If caught, both Anjali and Abdullah would face a barrage of questions, harassment and maybe arrest and imprisonment.

Anjali realized that Abdullah had taken this risk out of nicety; perhaps he couldn't refuse a former professor of his, a woman in distress who needed to be in a safe surrounding. She felt a surge of respect and gratitude well up in her eyes. It didn't go unnoticed by Abdullah, who smiled at her when she folded her hands as a mark of gratitude.

Very soon, they crossed a once pretty park now dotted with makeshift tents in tarpaulin. Men, women and babies were seen scattered around, sitting in twos and fours, staring blankly into nothingness. Children were playing in the dirt, tugging a used plastic bottle or a dirty soft toy. Some were busy cooking something in a pot. There was a huge line near a tap where dirty water was trickling down.

Abdullah explained that these were internally displaced people who had escaped the persecution of the Taliban in districts and villages. Perhaps they belonged to other ethnic groups like Tajiks and Hazaras; for the Taliban considers everyone who is not a Pashtun an enemy.

The family members of these people may have been killed or abducted, and they thought escaping to the city would ensure they went unnoticed and survived.

Anjali softly asked, 'Will they be unnoticed? Will they survive?'

Abdullah shook his head, 'That is very difficult to say, very difficult; no one knows. The soldiers are just waiting for their leaders to command them. Once they receive instructions, they will pounce on whoever they have been asked to attack. This is a state of utter lawlessness.

'I am a Pashtun—I might, just might, escape unharmed. However, Allah knows what is best for all of us. This is going to be a very dark phase for our country; not too sure how much worse it is going to get and what lies in store for us. Only Allah, the most merciful, knows about it.' Saying this, they both kept silent for the rest of the journey.

Perhaps in situations like this, it is better to be silent; no one has any answer, but lots of unanswered questions.

As they approached the embassy almost two hours later, Captain Varma was at the gate to usher in Anjali. He quickly came forward to take her backpack and greeted her.

'I am so happy you arrived safely.'

He shook hands with Abdullah and invited him for a cup of tea, which Abdullah politely declined. Anjali shook hands with Abdullah, invited him to India and promised to be in touch and meet again when better days resumed. As the gates of the Indian embassy closed behind Abdullah, Anjali walked towards the entrance of the building, finally feeling a bit secure and thanking Abdullah for his kindness in her heart.

◈

Back at the compound, everyone was preparing for the long and dangerous journey ahead. Cathy was instructing everyone as to what to say, what not to say and what to deny. She was running regular, rigorous drills with each of her friends, preparing them for every possibility, while Abdullah was busy procuring their visas and other documents they might need for the travel.

First, Abdullah procured hijabs for the women and a turban for Ayoub. Since Fawzia's son's looks clearly betrayed him and marked him as a Hazara boy, Abdullah got him a face mask and a shawl to cover him up; they would pretend that he was sick so that showing his face could be avoided at the check posts.

D-day was approaching, and when it finally arrived, it didn't look any different from the rest. The night before was long, and all those who were slated to undertake this journey tossed and turned in their bed, waking up several times drenched in sweat with a parched tongue and throat. Drinking from the bottle of water at their bedside till there was nothing left to drink. It was a never-ending night of torment, fear and apprehension. Stomachs churned and limbs were stiff at the mere thought of what lay ahead of them.

Finally, after a meagre breakfast and packing whatever food there was, Abdullah's car was sighted at the gate. Once he was with them, he explained that it wouldn't be possible for him to drive them towards Jalalabad. They would have to take a local vehicle, which had been arranged, and a few hundred dollars were given to them.

Ayoub and Zohra were to travel as a couple. A colleague of Abdullah, who would cross the border with them, would declare Nadia as his wife and Fawzia and her son as his sister and ailing nephew.

They had to be very careful about Cathy. She would have to travel fully covered through the journey so she wouldn't be recognized as a foreigner. And it was decided that, if, by any chance, her identity was revealed, she would pose as Zohra's Canadian mother.

Everybody was nervous and edgy. Cathy didn't want to take any chances this time and was going through the drill several times. Apprehension of the impending journey and the danger that lurked made them irritable. The cordiality that they once shared broke down. Zohra wanted to snap back many times, but her husband stopped her from losing her temper.

Abdullah introduced them to his colleague Shoaib, who was supposed to travel with them. He spoke to them and understood everyone's role and how he was supposed to act as Nadia's husband and Fawzia's brother.

At the embassy, Anjali received a warm welcome. Facilities were limited as it had never been built to accommodate so many people at the same time. She met a few women who had come to Kabul accompanying their husbands, engineers working on large construction projects.

She enjoyed being in the company of people from her own country, talking to them in Hindi, listening to their stories and sharing hers.

Anjali received a call from Jalaluddin. First, he sounded offended for not being informed about her move to the embassy. 'You should have told me. I could have driven you there. Do you still not trust me? Did you think I would take advantage of it and take you somewhere else? I would have safely seen you off at the embassy door.'

'It is not that; everything happened so fast. You know, after that night at the camp, I was not feeling safe. I just wanted to leave and go somewhere safe. I can go home from here, be on the evacuation flight back to India.'

'So, you are going back? Without meeting me, even once? I don't think I will be able to see you again. I am longing to catch a glimpse of you. If only you had told me, this could have been a lot easier for me. I, too, am slated to go back to the US. There won't be any common grounds or purpose to come together, I guess. Is this what you wanted? Tell me, honestly.'

The conversation carried on for some time. Anjali promised to call him before leaving Kabul.

The embassy officers did everything that they could to make everyone comfortable. Everyone was updated from time to time about the current scenario. They were on standby to be evacuated and taken to the airport as soon as the rescue flight arrived.

After two days, Nadia called Anjali and spoke to her at length about their preparation and onward journey. She was still nervous about her escapade, and Anjali tried her best to assure her of the brighter days ahead. She wasn't sure if these assurances helped, but she hoped this troubled girl's life would soon be better and safer.

Around two hundred people were waiting to be evacuated from Kabul at the embassy. People were loaded into a convoy of vehicles. Anjali was surprised to see that they were being escorted out by the Taliban soldiers, who appeared to be very polite, and some of them also smiled and waved at them. Her questioning glance was understood by Captain Varma.

'We had to get their help. There are new checkpoints, and some roads have been blocked. There is firing and chaos, without their help, we will not be able to reach the airport.'

'And they decided to help? That's surprising.' The last question of Anjali was unanswered.

The three-mile road to the airport took more than four hours to reach. But no one was worried about missing their flight, it was an army plane of the Indian Air Force.

As Anjali sat in the car, the road beneath her rattling, her phone lit up. Jalaluddin's number flashed on her screen. 'Hi, how are you? How are you feeling?' floated his usual question in a soft lilt.

'I know you are probably on your way home. Probably this will be the last time you came to our country. I don't think you will ever come back again.'

Anjali was taken aback by his forthrightness, 'No. No, that is not the case. I was preoccupied with so many things. The arrangements ... too many things on my mind.'

'And I didn't feature in that mind of yours ...'

Anjali kept quiet while Jalal continued, 'Next time we meet, it will be a better situation. I promise. I will bring a gift, something you like. Please remain in touch. I am not good with words. I shall pray for your safety. Alhamdulillah, you will be home soon.'

Anjali sighed as she cut the call and kept the phone in her handbag. Several thoughts crossed her mind. Would she meet Jalal again? Would they talk? Did she do the right thing? She remembered Jalal's voice, his laughter and his large frame. A part of her felt hollow. She should have been happy that she was now going home, but she didn't. She felt sad and lonely. She tried hard to fight back her tears.

As the vehicles reached the airport, one could see thousands of people lined up outside the gate. Desperation was written all across their faces. Once the people from the Indian embassy moved slowly towards their flight, some people looked sad, as if their eyes were pleading to take them. The dust and dirt at the airport signified the hopelessness of this beautiful country.

Everyone lined up to fill the belly of the C-17 aircraft, which would take the people back to their motherland. A few enthusiastic people chanted 'Bharat Mata ki jai' and 'Vande Mataram' and the sentiment was echoed with renewed fervour.

Anjali, tying her seatbelt, looked out of the window. For the last time to see dust flying amidst chaos, the last image of Kabul. She was supposed to be here for the next year as per her contract. She was to befriend people from this country. Life could have been different, but it was not.

This is what was meant to be, and this is what has happened. Abhay was not to be; he was not there. She was still breathing, and she wanted to be grateful for it. She closed her eyes and reclined her head on the uncomfortable seat.

All left behind, the campus, the students, colleagues, Jalal, the mountains, the dusty roads, the oily rice in the canteen. Her belongings in her container, everything left behind as a part of her in the form of her memories, in this godforsaken land, forever.

The flight took the people to the western part of India, from Jamnagar, and then to Hindon air base. There were tears of relief. People hugged each other, and a few women came to hug Anjali too, which she warmly reciprocated. Passenger flights would be arranged to take people back to their respective homes.

As Anjali walked down, clutching her handbag, for the first time after a long gap, she felt empty. Something was missing and would never return to her life. This is what she felt when she was in the car after Abhay's funeral, coming back home alone.

She didn't want to switch on her mobile. She knew no one was waiting anymore to eagerly hear her voice and get excited about her homecoming. She walked slowly, not in a hurry to go anywhere, head down, carefully measuring her steps. She had left Kabul, but she didn't know what awaited her next.

12

The visas that Abdullah procured had aliases and inaccurate information. But no one cared; this document was their ticket to freedom, and all six of them clutched them tight. They left the camp around seven in the morning, after a frugal breakfast of toast and tea.

Cathy went to meet the commander and exchanged email IDs and phone numbers. He came towards the gate with them and urged them to write back once they reached a place of safety. He, too, was planning to head home to Canada and was busy arranging it.

As planned, the women donned burqas leaving only their eyes uncovered. Fawzia's son was wrapped in a shawl and a face mask.

The vehicle sent by Abdullah was ready to take them to Jalalabad. Abdullah called and instructed them once more about things to be said and things that were not supposed to be uttered. As everyone got into the jeep Abdullah had arranged, everyone muttered a prayer and braced themselves for a long journey.

The first part of the journey was uneventful. The road started getting rocky, and the vehicle would very often plunge into a pothole, jerk and get back on the road again. The dust was choking everyone, and their mouths felt sandy and coarse. Water bottles were used sparsely. Several times, hands reached out for water to moisten their tongues and lips or splash a bit on their eyes, which were becoming red and runny with dust.

Fawzia's son, bundled in a shawl, was feeling sick, and the car had to stop because he wanted to throw up. Fawzia was getting worried; this was just the start of a long journey, and she needed her son to be well.

Everyone maintained a sombre look, followed by silence; there was nothing much to discuss. Suddenly, they hit a traffic snarl; it seemed everyone was using the same route to escape out of the country. Vehicles loaded with bags, people with parents, families with kids, newly married couples and young children were sitting patiently inside the cars with blank expressions on their faces. The air was thick with apprehension.

A sense of foreboding was in the air; something was going to happen. What would happen, when it might happen and what would be the degree of its impact were not known to anyone.

Fawzia's son was gagging with violent coughs that shook his tender frame. No amount of water, sweets or even cough drops were helping him. The car had to stop at the side, allowing him to throw up again.

Fawzia's forehead was wrinkled with worry. Nadia tried to assure her while Zohra was trying to fetch some toffees for the child. Cathy was visibly irritated with the child. She kept making a clucking noise, 'He must stop coughing so loudly, we will get caught. He is drawing attention to the vehicle. The journey is getting delayed. We need to cross before the sun sets today.'

She sounded determined and merciless. It seemed that she would not allow anything to get in her way of reaching the border and crossing over, even if it meant sacrifices. Everyone stiffened as they heard and saw the ruthless side of a once-benevolent teacher.

The driver started speaking to Ayoub, as men in this country rarely address or discuss important things with women, especially in this new regime. He suggested that the vehicle should abandon this route and try to move to the countryside where the pollution was less and the dust was not so bothersome. Perhaps he thought this would help Fawzia's little boy. The route might take them a bit longer, but it would be better for everyone. After a brief discussion, while not everyone was on board, it was decided that a detour would be best for all.

This route was more pleasant; the countryside was lined with orange trees where blossoms could be seen sprouting. The countryside was a balm to their anxious souls. The car halted after some time so everyone could stretch their legs.

A small boy came running to sell some bolani, and everyone bought one and munched happily. Cathy, though, not really pleased with the deviation from the decided path, politely refused and kept to her supply of apples.

Fawzia's son felt a lot better, and the colour started returning to his cheeks. His mother heaved a sigh of relief.

After the break, the group piled into the car and braced for the final leg of the journey. The car now joined the convoy of other cars, inching slowly towards Jalalabad. The journey was slow and tedious, but there was hope at the end of the journey. Everyone's bodies were tense with apprehension, sitting on the edge, as if ready to run towards their freedom if anything untoward happened.

There were no check posts on the way. The cars coiled and moved in unison with each other as if following a set pattern patiently. Zohra saw a crowded vehicle with its windows rolled up and no air-conditioning, pass by. It certainly didn't look like a pleasant ride, but the promise of the future made them endure.

Nearly three hours passed before they reached Jalalabad.

It was a bright day, and everyone had just one thought on their mind now—how were they going to be smuggled inside a truck in broad daylight, out in the open? Shouldn't they be going to a warehouse instead of standing here where hundreds of cars were passing by? Surely, being sighted would be catastrophic, and the plan to get across would fail.

Cathy dialled Abdullah's number to figure this out before everyone broke into a full-blown panic.

Nadia moaned, 'What calamity has befallen us, Allah! Why are we always subjected to such torture? Is our country ever going to witness peace and prosperity?'

No one had any answer to her questions; over forty years of civil war had made everyone exhausted and resigned to fate.

Abdullah answered his phone after two rings.

His voice on the other end was a bit hesitant. 'There has been a change of plans. I am sorry about that. I think smuggling you into the truck would be very risky. If you are found out, then there would be no questioning, no interrogation, but straight beheading. It is way too risky.

'On top of it, I would not be spared, and my eldest son has just become a father. I am still in the hospital. As much as I care for your safety, I care for my family's safety, too.

'I am sorry. But, no, I am not abandoning you at all. I will see to it that this journey is completed.'

He continued with new instructions. 'There is a roadside eatery near where you are called Jannat-e-Dawat. The journey ahead will be tedious, and you all must be hungry. Please do go and eat something, and I will send a car to pick you all up. You will reach Peshawar before night falls. That is my promise.'

While everyone was uncomfortable with this sudden change of plans, there was no scope, no allowance now to negotiate. What was suggested by Abdullah had to be heeded; they were at his mercy, and time was running out.

Although none of them had any appetite, Ayoub spoke to the driver, and they headed for the restaurant. Calling it a restaurant would be an exaggeration. It was a small, stand-alone shop with a tin shade. These kinds of eateries were popular in the countryside.

Ayoub went and spoke to the man handling the cash. He urged them to find a seat inside as there were women with him. This was a sentiment that was well understood by everyone in this country. They were ushered in, and a table in the corner was shown to them. There were six red plastic chairs, a garish colourful plastic tablecloth and a plastic jug.

A man came towards them, rubbing his hand on the checkered cloth kept on his shoulder. His pencil was delicately balanced on the upper lobe of his ear, which he fished out along with a small notebook. Ayoub ordered a dish of mutton keema (minced meat) and naan (bread). The order was repeated by everyone, except for Cathy, who just ordered a cup of green tea.

Cathy looked around and commented, 'I suppose they don't have a washroom for women. This place is filthy. The smell of fried things hangs heavily in the air. I just don't want to fall sick before I land in Peshawar.'

Not much was discussed; others hungrily grabbed the food. Fawzia was busy helping her son with the food while Cathy kept quiet, occasionally sipping her tea. Managing the hijab and the burqa, and yet having her tea, was quite a challenge for her.

Some curious onlookers noticed them, but no one was inclined to talk or ask any questions. There was a weary look on everybody's face. A few families were sitting away from them: the father organizing food and the mother busy feeding the little ones. Some women had put out their feeding bottles, which were getting filled with warm milk, perhaps a ration for their onward journey.

Apart from the children who were busy playing in the dirt, running around the plastic chairs and giggling, the adults wore worried looks. Perhaps they wanted the next leg of the journey to be as peaceful and trouble-free as this one.

After a while, Abdullah walked into the restaurant. It seemed that people around here were familiar with him, and the cashier got up to greet him. He ordered a chai and came over to the table where they were seated.

He wanted to know how their journey had been so far and asked in detail as to what they saw, whom they interacted with and what the condition of the road was. Ayoub, who by now had taken on the role of being the guide and the pathfinder of the group, briefed him. Abdullah turned towards Fawzia and enquired about her son's well-being.

He then turned around to address everyone about the final leg of their journey. Clearing his throat, he remarked, 'I am so glad that till now all went well. The minor detour is okay; we need to adjust our journey as we try to manoeuvre our way towards safety. I thank Allah for guiding us and taking us on the desired route towards freedom.

'I had to abandon the idea of the truck as it would have been too risky. I would need the help of my workers, the loaders, the driver and the helper. Way too many people would be involved, and this is a time when we can't trust anyone. Hence, I have arranged for a vehicle that will take you across the border.

'The driver is a trusted man, and he has been paid enough to undertake this journey. You will all pretend to be family, know each other and cross the border. Remember to keep the visas with you. And ladies, please don't remove your burqa, you must always wear them.

'This route, although short, is risky; the mountainous roads are dangerous. The Talibs are fiercely guarding the entire road, and there are several checkpoints. I am told that they are segregating people who sound dubious or are unable to furnish their papers. I have no clue about their fate, perhaps they are taken into some obscure prison.'

Abdullah paused to breathe; he was clearly agitated, talking about arrests and prisons.

Cathy asked the most important question, 'What if we are caught? What if we are segregated and imprisoned, what will happen to us?' She sounded nervous, and her voice quivered.

Abdullah started talking now, almost in a whisper.

'I have no idea, Dr Cathy. I have no idea. I only hope and pray that such calamity doesn't befall any of us. I can give you all a car, I can give you food to eat, mineral water to drink, but what I cannot assure you is safe passage.'

He looked at her seriously. 'Again, I can only pray for it. I won't be able to do anything if you get caught or imprisoned.'

Ayoub came forward and placed his hand on Abdullah's shoulder, 'You have done enough for us. We owe our lives to you. You bailed us out of the kidnapping, paying a large amount of money. You procured our visas; you managed to take us to Jalalabad. Now you are giving us a car and driver to take us to Peshawar. No one would have done so much for us, not now in this state of crisis.

'We will never be able to repay your loan; it is not just monetary. You have a newborn angel in your household, such an occasion of joy. Yet, you are here standing with us, having travelled several kilometres, we don't have enough words to thank you.'

Saying this, Ayoub got emotional and hugged Abdullah.

It seemed that this would be their last meeting with Abdullah. The air was heavy with emotion, voices were choked and the corners of their eyes glistened. Even little Arzoo came to touch Abdullah's hand, and he patted his cheeks.

Cathy spoke softly, 'Abdullah, you did a lot for this teacher of yours. I just taught a few lessons, but I learned kindness from you. I may have demanded more than you gave, but you gave it uncomplainingly. I also hope that someday I can repay this loan. I am grateful that our paths crossed in this country. I hope to meet you again.'

After goodbyes and a few more tips to complete the last leg of the journey, Abdullah left in his car. He assured them that in less than half an hour, the car would be there to take them across the border. The group sat inside the restaurant and waited for the car to come.

13

No need to rush or worry about food, accommodation, escape, vehicle, roads or the airport. These were Anjali's thoughts when she woke up the next morning, having reached her home in Delhi late last evening.

She looked around. It was her home, her bed and her photographs on the wall opposite. The painting that she and her husband had chosen so lovingly looked nice and colourful. Everything was familiar, everything was warm and safe.

She sat for two minutes hugging her knees on the bed, trying to acclimatize and soak in the fact that she was back in her own country, her own home. There was still disbelief lurking in her mind. She kept wondering whether she had been able to come back unharmed and untouched.

The morning sun was still mild and peeped from behind the curtains. She decided to sit near the window with her favourite cup of Darjeeling tea brewed in the consistency that she preferred.

On a whim, she dialled Jalaluddin's number. He was quick to pick it up, and his voice floated from a far and distant land, yet a place where she was only yesterday. 'Thank you for calling. I am so glad to see your number flash across my screen. I am thankful to Allah that you are safe and have reached home. How are you feeling? Are you tired?'

There was an awkward silence, a bit of stammering, a long pause and breathing noises. There was so much to be said, so much was unspoken, but no one gathered the courage to voice it. It hung from the tip of their lips but could never be realized.

Again, a polite goodbye, a flimsy promise to keep in touch, and the phone call ended with a sigh, an unfinished business that was perhaps slated to fade into the horizon even before it blossomed.

Anjali got up lethargically. She splashed some water on her face and went about unpacking her belongings. While stowing away her clothes, she once again touched the ones belonging to Abhay and hung them beside her own. It felt real, it felt like his skin, and it smelled of him. She drew a deep breath as if to soak in his smell and closed the cupboard. The precious memories remained locked in her bosom. She decided to go about her life as if the dark phase never existed.

◈

At Jalalabad, the group kept waiting in anticipation; now and then, one would go to the main road to see whether any empty vehicle was in sight. After an hour, Ayoub spotted a white SUV approaching the restaurant. This vehicle was unassuming, a bit dilapidated, and looked like it needed repair.

No time was wasted, and they all climbed into it. They huddled on the seats, which were covered with some old rugs. Visas were checked, money was hidden inside shirts and blouses, hijabs were adjusted, and they were all set to complete the last and most dangerous path to escape.

Very soon, they joined a long convoy of cars, buses and trucks. The narrow, winding, hilly track had no by-lanes. They had no alternative but to join the long queue.

The waiting was endless, and everyone was visibly tense about the approaching checkpoint. It took them four hours to reach the check post at the border.

As they all saw the first man approach the vehicle, their hearts started racing. He was a tall, lanky guy in his twenties, with a white cloth wrapped around his head and the telltale signs of long hair, kohl-rimmed eyes and a Kalashnikov on his shoulder. He came towards the window and put his hand inside the car, demanding to see their papers. Ayoub gingerly handed it over. After the man went through the papers, he started talking rapidly in Pashto and wanted to know who they were, what their relationships were and where they were heading. Ayoub explained that they were all related; his wife was pregnant and not keeping well, and his aunt Fawzia's son was gravely ill, and they were heading towards Peshawar for proper treatment.

The curious man wanted to know about the masked child then. Ayoub explained his ailment and that he was still undiagnosed, and that he was losing weight rapidly. The man seemed to be kind; he nodded his head and kept saying 'Allah Khair' (May God help him).

Everyone else in the car was stiff with apprehension and kept their eyes averted. Zohra looked at her husband with admiration as he negotiated with the soldiers of the Taliban.

As the cars started moving slowly, everyone turned to see whether he was talking on his radio and informing the others ahead. A collective sigh of relief rose in the car as they saw him move on to the next car. But the relief was temporary.

Very soon, just as they were half a metre away from the check post, two of the soldiers asked them to take the car to the corner of the road.

Nadia let out a small cry, and Zohra clutched Cathy's hand very tightly, digging her nails into her palm. Fawzia started shielding her son with her two hands as if her palms could make him invisible. Only Ayoub looked calm and composed. He muttered under his breath to himself that there was no point in disobeying or arguing; they would be gunned down on the spot.

The driver nervously steered the car towards the side and parked it. He, too, was visibly sweating and his face was turning red. Fear gripped everyone inside the car as they slowly alighted and stood with their backs to the car. The two rough-looking soldiers asked the women to move away to one side, while the men were asked to accompany them.

Zohra started crying helplessly; she didn't want Ayoub to disappear from her sight. The men heard her and came to shout at her, asking her to stop the useless wail. Nadia too started sobbing. Cathy, who read the situation better than everyone, whispered loudly under her breath for them to keep quiet and not to exhibit their fear.

Ayoub and the driver started walking with the guards, and the women stood rooted to the ground. Moments passed, and no one knew what was going to happen to them. They were paralysed with fear and apprehension. Vehicles kept passing by, and some people looked out of the window with sympathy in their eyes. Everyone knew that alighting from the car meant consequences; it meant trouble lay ahead for them.

Thirty minutes, forty-five minutes, a whole hour passed, and still there was no sign of Ayoub. Zohra feared the worst; she flopped on the road, sitting there like a lifeless person. Nadia, too, sat down beside her, and Fawzia followed with her son. Stripped of their dignity, they sat on the road, simply staring at the passing vehicles. Only Cathy stood upright, leaning on the car.

Nadia started rocking and mumbling to herself, 'I am the cursed one. My father died after I was born. My marriage didn't work; I shamed my family, my brothers and my mother. They will carry this burden on their shoulders forever. The house whose daughter ran away. It is not going to stop.

'My husband will hunt me down and kill me. Perhaps from here, we will be dragged to some prison where we will be tortured to death, hanged in public or even stoned to death. This is it; this was what was meant to happen to a cursed woman who couldn't stay with her husband. Who couldn't resign to Allah's will, who wanted to make her world of luxury and success? I am greedy, I should die, only death should be my punishment.'

This time, Zohra or Fawzia didn't have the capability to soothe her, their anxiety crippling them into silence. They kept looking at her blankly with tears streaking down their faces, as they had by now lifted the veil covering their faces.

All this was too much for Cathy, too. She turned around and let out a sharp growl.

'Stop it, stop it, Nadia! If you cannot muster the courage to face this situation, then you should have stayed at home and listened to your husband. You should have been his sex slave or whatever you call it. It is only about you, your fear, your pain, your shame, nothing about us. I have had enough of this.

'I have come this far because of two monsters in my life who robbed me of my child, my money and my dignity. Then I trusted a university with lofty sayings that literally threw us on the road and ran away. What do we do? Should we join you and squat on the road and start rocking and wailing like you?'

Nadia stopped and looked at her in amazement. She had not expected such an outburst. Fawzia kept her head down, and Zohra kept nodding her head in disapproval, but didn't say anything.

Fawzia's son, who was standing aside quietly, started urinating in his pants in fear, and weeping. Fawzia, in anger, tried to slap him, but Zohra stopped her hand midway.

'It's not his fault; he is not well. It is too much for us, and he is so little. Think about him. Take him to the other side of the car and take a pair of fresh trousers and change him. Be careful on the other side of the car. These are evil times. No one is spared.'

Fawzia nodded her head in agreement and took Arzoo for a change.

A silence followed. It was a hostile silence. The flight to safety had taken a toll on each of them. They were bearing each other's company and wishing every moment that they could be on their own. Everyone had only one thought in mind: they wanted this ordeal to end. Somehow.

Zohra got up and dusted her jeans and said, 'This is too much to take—no food, no sleep, out on the roads and the fear of being caught and killed, how much more?' Was it a prayer, as she looked up at the sky?

Perhaps it was a prayer. Just then, they all saw Ayoub crossing the road with the driver. He looked exhausted and drained but was smiling. He dodged the lines of the car and came in front of them.

He smiled. 'It's done. I managed to convince them. It seems I am a good storyteller. The last hurdle has been crossed, and all visas have been stamped.'

He laughed, 'Zohra, no, you cannot hug me in the middle of the road!'

They got into the car, and everyone thanked Ayoub for being a saviour and bailing them out of impending imprisonment and death. They wanted to know what transpired and how he convinced the soldiers.

The car joined the convoy and crossed the checkpoint. The Afghans looked back, catching a glimpse of their beloved country for the last time.

It was Fawzia who said aloud what all of them were thinking, 'When will we come back. Will we come back?'

No one had the answer; they all drove on in silence.

14

Slowly, the convoy moved towards Peshawar. It was evening by the time they crossed the border to Pakistan and entered Peshawar. Having left the Nangarhar province in Afghanistan, the cars were now in the Khyber Pakhtunkhwa province on the Pakistani side.

Abdullah's distant cousin ran a lodging in the Qissa Khwani Bazaar, a densely populated area of old Peshawar. The lodging, like many others, was called 'Jannat' and in no way resembled heaven, but could be a haven for all those who had escaped the brutal rule that was now settling down once again in Afghanistan.

The driver dialled a number, and an elderly gentleman dressed in a traditional shalwar and a skull cap came to meet them. He introduced himself as Mohammad and was yet another distant cousin of Abdullah. As they climbed up an old staircase painted in garish blue, he apologized for not having separate rooms for all.

He just had a large room with two beds and requested everyone to accommodate themselves.

'People are coming in hundreds and thousands. Some are with their ailing parents or a newborn baby. Allah! Have mercy on us. They have left everything behind; they hardly have a sack on their back.

'We open our doors to everyone, house them and give them food to eat, even if they can't pay. Allah is all merciful. He monitors everything. He will give justice to all.'

One room was good enough; the exhausted passengers were not left with much choice. It was a barren room with two rickety beds and a table with a plastic water jug, and it opened to a noisy balcony on the road. The washroom was sordid and needed thorough cleaning. Cathy sighed as she looked around. Zohra tried to check the silky floral bedcover but then decided against it.

The driver who was carrying their luggage now took their leave. He would stay back at his cousin's place for the night and drive back to Jalalabad to complete some errands that Abdullah had assigned him to do. A phone call was made to Abdullah in his presence and Cathy thanked him profusely.

Apart from a slow-paced whizzing fan, the room was hot and claustrophobic. Ayoub opened the door leading to the balcony. The room was filled with the sound of cars honking on the road below and the smell of food being cooked in the makeshift stalls on the road.

Mohammad looked embarrassed and added politely, 'There is not much we can do. It is a hard time. Let me get some food for you all. Naan and kebab? And green tea? Sounds good? I will try and get a glass of hot milk for the boy.'

It was decided that the women and the little boy would try to squeeze onto the bed, and Ayoub would spread a sheet on the floor and sleep. It was just a matter of one night.

Mohammad came back with some food on pink printed paper. He placed it on the low table at the centre of the room.

Before he left, he cleared his throat and said, 'Just be cautious. Many Pashtuns work as informers for the Taliban; they stay here or in the vicinity. They monitor and report back. Don't indulge in small talk. Remain safe till you are on your way to Islamabad tomorrow morning.'

Saying this, he looked straight at Nadia, nodded his head and went away. Nadia rushed to bolt the door as soon as he left.

The night remained uneventful. They dug into the tasteless food and splashed some water on themselves from the wash basin to get rid of all the dirt and grime settled on them. They all tried to get as much rest as possible before the next leg of their journey.

In the wee hours of dawn, with the call for prayer on the microphone, everyone was up and about, busy preparing for yet another journey ahead. Some tea and bread, a quick packing of their bags and the charging of their phones. By 9 a.m., they were on the streets. Mohammad had procured tickets for them; the bus ride would be less than two hours, and the tickets were cheap, less than twenty dollars.

After a while, a bus came—one of those minivans which could take around twenty people. The bus had a fancy name, 'Henna', and was well decorated in the front. Ayoub shook hands with Mohammad and thanked him for his hospitality. Everyone took turns thanking him and boarded the bus. Yet another ride and a new destination.

The bus was filled with Afghans who were all on their way to Islamabad. A child was crying incessantly; the father looked around and apologetically said that he had a high fever and there were no signs of remission. The conversation was followed by tut-tuts and clucking sounds and some unwanted advice. The ride remained uneventful.

The bus reached the destination, and everyone alighted. Nadia was emotional; she kept hugging Zohra, Fawzia and little Arzoo. Cathy was distant but shook hands with everyone and patted little Arzoo on his cheeks.

Ayoub suggested that they should go to the nearby coffee shop and have a cup each for the last time. The cafe across the street was inviting, well-decorated and clean. They all went inside. There was no more rushing, no hurry, no escaping. They sat down with a sigh of relief and munched on cream cones and sipped a frothy cup of coffee each.

Cathy asked, 'Where do you all plan to go from here? I have contacted my embassy, and I will head there straight. I will stay for a few days and fly back home. Flights are regular; I just need to get the visa done, whatever time it takes. But I was told it will be an express one, so maybe two or three days.'

Zohra spoke, 'We will also go to the Canadian embassy. Mine is a case of going back home, but we need to apply for Ayoub's Canadian visa. My parents have agreed to help; hence, he will be sponsored.

'I don't think it should take much time, maybe a fortnight. Till then, we will stay in a cheap hotel. Money is a bit tight, but I always have my wedding ring. Ayoub, won't you get me another one if this needs to be sold?' she chuckled, and Ayoub smiled with approval.

Fawzia had contacted her ex-husband's cousin, who stayed in Islamabad and worked in a hospital. 'He will come, he promised. We stay there and then go to Doha.'

Nadia didn't know anyone and was afraid to reach out to anybody, lest they tell her husband. She turned to Fawzia, 'Fawzia Jan, can I stay with you for the time being? I promise I will not pose any problem. I have contacted my ex-professor. She will take me to Doha and then to another country where I can study and complete my degree. She is working out the details.

'She said there will be loads of paperwork to be done since I have no guardian. I am sorry, but I don't feel safe alone, hiring a hotel room.' Fawzia looked at her with kindness and said, 'Sure, I will explain it to my brother-in-law. You are welcome.'

Cathy put the cup on the plate noisily and said, 'All right then, that settles it. We go our different ways from here. No more tied to a cause, the cause of escaping. We had a good time together. Destiny brought us together, and we spent many a tense moment together.

'The camp, the roads and my mistake of trying to escape with all of you, all seem to be a distant past. A dream now that is slowly fading into a fuzzy mist.

'I won't promise to keep in touch—I am bad at it. But if we work or remain connected to the university, our paths will surely cross. God bless you all.'

Having paid the bill, they came out and stood on the porch. The sun was bright, and it was slightly breezy. Cathy tucked her hair behind her ears and took a deep breath.

'Ah! The smell of freedom. I am addicted to this smell. This is the third time that I can take a deep breath, having earned my freedom, once again.'

They shook hands, hugged each other and went on their way. Some looked for a taxi, some hailed a bus and some stood on the spot dialling a number for a pickup.

The escape, came to an end in another country. A country that assured them the freedom to walk around, breathe and choose their destination. An escape from death, an escape from humiliation and an escape from the throbbing apprehension of getting caught.

Part VI

BADAN CHI SHOD? WHAT HAPPENED NEXT?

15

Cathy went back to her home. The first few days, she stayed with her mother and then got a place of her own, a nice little studio apartment. She wrote a blog about her escape, and she published it on social media. It attracted many readers; people were hungry to know what was happening in Afghanistan.

The current regime had imposed an embargo on the foreign press. Journalists started reaching out to her to paint a picture of the country and its future. She became an analyst and commentator on Afghan politics and the interim government. Her interview was aired on several media channels.

The board of trustees of the university decided to honour her and gave her a promotion. The teaching staff, who had now started teaching online, was to report to her. She was managing quality control, teaching load allocation and managing online schedules, all at once.

She was happy. She was happy with her success, the money, the position and the power. She just didn't have the time to keep in touch with her fellow escapees.

She was now negotiating with some Islamic nations to create a refuge and haven for the students. She was dealing with diplomats and travelling to other countries as the guest of honour and was invited to speak about her contribution to rescuing people.

She was amassing large amounts of donations from funding bodies. She created a website that would help uplift poor, vulnerable girls from Afghanistan who needed money. However, it was a different story that the money was always parked in someone's personal account in a safe country.

Despite the shared experience and struggle, she was not interested in knowing how Fawzia was struggling or whether Zohra got the visa for Ayoub. It was as if she had pushed away everything that had happened then, and her escape was just a story for her now.

Back in India, Anjali needed a break, and the break came in the form of a cousin's wedding. She decided to immerse herself in it fully. Her days were filled with laughter, festivity, music, marriage rituals and dressing up once again. Her family members were happy for her and encouraged her to be a part of every celebration.

The university reached out to her to resume her work and teach online. She refused but decided to teach one course a semester just to stay in touch with teaching and the curriculum. She joined an NGO that worked with slum children and worked part-time with their strategy team. The money was paltry, but the satisfaction was immense, and it kept her busy and happy.

She met Cathy online a couple of times when all the faculty members met to exchange notes. They avoided each other and behaved like strangers.

There were a few instances when Jalal and Anjali exchanged pleasantries. After a while, Jalal was in Pakistan and then flew to the US on an 'academic refugee scholarship programme'. He enrolled in the prestigious Woodford University and kept himself busy narrating the history and the future of the Taliban rule in Afghanistan. He was seen online in several webinars in a crisp white shirt, wearing a thick gold chain and keeping nicely trimmed beard and hair, sporting a pair of Ray-Ban sunglasses, talking about how miserable he was and how he managed to escape from being brought to the gallows. The narrative was the same as the last day on campus, a sleepy soliloquy that never went in any direction.

Several messages from Anjali remained unanswered.

A colleague offered to help Anjali find out what had happened. She forwarded a voice message from Jalaluddin.

'Oh! Fatima, don't worry. There was nothing serious about us. *Tauba*. She was my colleague, and I respected her. Oh, those text messages and the visit. First, it was COVID, then it was the Taliban. I could hardly go out of the house. I was bored, and this was a good way to pass my time. No, I don't know anything about her. I heard she is no longer at the university. What is the point of keeping in touch with her? No longer a senior colleague of mine. She can't be of any use to me. I think I might seek a pretty blond girl here who will help me get American citizenship. What do you think?' The conversation ended with a burst of wholehearted laughter.

Anjali heard the voice message, smiled and kept the phone away. The gush of emotions from Jalal and his love-coated messages, sometimes in hundreds, was too fragile to last. Perhaps, in her heart, she knew this was how this would end.

Zohra's struggles didn't end. She had to run from pillar to post to get her husband a Canadian visa. She would visit the embassy almost daily and sometimes twice a day. Ayoub reached out to his mother, who refused to talk to him, and he could only brief his father about his whereabouts.

Zohra pawned her trinkets to keep paying for the hotel and visa fees. Ultimately, she reached out to her parents. After an episode of scolding, crying and being upset with each other, her father agreed to help her. He sponsored Ayoub as his only son-in-law. He took care of the paperwork, and very soon they flew to Canada.

Back in Canada, Zohra resumed her studies and her rigorous sports practice. Ayoub, after getting acclimatized to the new culture, got a job as an accountant with a law firm. They rented a small apartment and decided to have a family very soon. Ayoub tried to make peace with his mother and hoped someday he would be able to do so.

Fawzia remained confined to a small room in Islamabad for a month or so; calling it a room would be an exaggeration. Her ex-husband's cousin could only make some space in the storeroom. She, Arzoo and Nadia squeezed in amidst old pots and pans and discarded furniture. She helped in the household and got meals for free, for which she was grateful.

In the meantime, she made several rounds of the visa office, going to a cyber cafe, and with the help of Nadia, sending several emails and scanned documents. Nadia was busy doing her bit, too. The NGO that promised Fawzia a job in Ireland was trying its best to move her from Islamabad. They finally succeeded, and Fawzia was slated to make her journey to a Middle Eastern country where she was to be housed for a few days.

On the designated day, she bade farewell to Nadia, the family that helped her and, holding little Arzoo, she arrived at a makeshift camp. The room allocated to her was comfortable, complete with a bed and a writing table. They got all three meals a day and three hundred dollars as dole money. The 'few days' became a month and then two; Fawzia was caught in endless red tape. She didn't have a school degree, her divorce papers were missing, her birth certificate was obscure, and her passport was not enough.

It seemed her Ireland dream had to be stalled for some time. She secured a job in an office canteen and, hobbling on her crutch and her wooden leg, she started going to work regularly.

Private schools were out of reach, and the public schools had Arabic as a mandatory language. She kept aside a portion of her income and arranged private tuition for Arzoo so that he could learn Arabic and get into a school the next year.

She got used to the hot and dry weather of the Middle East. She had picked up their cuisine and could speak a word or two in Arabic. She looked for a small apartment where she could stay with her son. The makeshift refugee camp could never be a permanent solution. She sent a hundred dollars to her parents, and they were happy about it.

When she spread her prayer mat in the evening and knelt to pray, she thanked the Almighty for all that he had given her. It was a lot, and she could only be grateful for it. She always knelt in reverence and prayed to remain self-sufficient and bring up her son as a good human being.

Nadia left the makeshift apartment a few days after Fawzia flew to the Middle East. Fawzia's relatives were kind and kept her for a few days. They, too, were concerned that a young and pretty girl like Nadia would not be comfortable and safe in a hotel or a guest house.

The university was in touch with Nadia, and they placed her in a bachelor's degree programme at a university in Central Asia. Nadia wanted to reach out to her family to share the news, but was warned by her friend Breshna. It seemed that her husband had created a ruckus and blamed her family for getting him married to a 'fallen woman'.

He was preparing for yet another marriage to a teenager from the village who had never learned to read or write. He approached the village council and divorced Nadia in her absence. Breshna was also scared of his wrath, and Nadia now kept in touch with her using a pseudo email ID called 'The American Girl'.

Some days, when Nadia stood in front of the mirror and adjusted her hijab over her thick chestnut hair, she quietly let her fingers caress them. Then she would think that one day, maybe one day, she would be able to let her hair down and run through a vast meadow and let the wind play with her hair. When she would come home, she would stand in front of the mirror and pick the grass blades that had deliberately chosen her hair in which to get stuck.

Today, she was happy that she could study again; perhaps at the end of the year, she would get a degree and maybe pursue a master's programme. This life was a privilege that so many like her had been denied.

The world comes to rest, and the fading sunlight bids its farewell with a promise that tomorrow will be a better day. This is a promise that keeps the hope of so many girls alive in the remote corners of mountainous Afghanistan. They will flourish again, go to universities and earn their degrees. While they pick up their child and start kneading the dough for dinner, they smile to themselves and say, 'This too shall pass.'

Acknowledgements

I have not learned how to thank my soul, hence a thank you to my late husband, Vijay Kapur, sounds banal. He is the reason behind everything that I do or create. My parents, Mira and Naresh Ranjan Sengupta, continue to bless me from where they are. My sister, Nilakshi Sengupta, hasn't stopped being the overprotective and indulgent sister since the day she picked me up in her arms.

I am thankful to my student, Ali Maher, for helping me with the translation of certain phrases in Dari. I am also thankful to my two other students, Rizwanullah Bahrami and Nawida Faizy, for narrating their journey from Kabul to Peshawar through the Torkham border crossing.

I would like to thank Engineer Aruel Diaz, who helped me fill up the gaps with his own narration and experience about his escape from Kabul.

Suhail Mathur, my literary agent at The Book Bakers, thank you for your continuous support.

I thank Ms Bushra Ahmed, my commissioning editor from HarperCollins, who was always beside me, correcting and suggesting changes. I felt most comfortable while brainstorming with her to improve what I wrote.

This life is a blessing, and I am grateful to everyone who helped me sail through it. Every day, I hope and pray that my friends from Afghanistan are safe and have started breathing once again. I get invitations to come back and visit their beautiful country. I am sure that I will, someday, soon.

This book is dedicated to the beautiful and resilient people of Afghanistan who embraced me and continue to love me as their own.

About the Author

Enakshi Sengupta is the CEO and founder of Borders without Barbed Wires, an NGO that promotes cross-border education in emergencies among marginalized and vulnerable communities. She has close to three decades of experience working in both the corporate world and an academic environment. She holds a PhD and an MBA degree from the University of Nottingham.

Enakshi has been honoured with several international awards, including Reading the Author Award for Best Debut Novel, 2025, and the University of Nottingham Alumni Award for Excellence in Arts, Culture and Creativity, 2024. She has contributed to several international journals and books published by Routledge, Springer, Palgrave, Cambridge, among others. Her debut novel, *The Silk Route Spy*, received widespread acclaim.